—— The Leg
CASEY
BROTHERS

JIM HUDSON WITH JIM CASEY

The Collins Press

FIRST PUBLISHED IN PAPERBACK IN 2013 BY
The Collins Press
West Link Park
Doughcloyne
Wilton
Cork

First published in hardback 1991

Paperback ISBN: 978-1848891838
PDF eBook ISBN: 9781848898233
EPUB eBook ISBN: 9781848898240
Kindle ISBN: 9781848898257

Typesetting by Carrigboy Typesetting Services
Typeset in Garamond Premier Pro
Printed in Malta by Gutenberg Press Limited

CONTENTS

FOREWORD

by WEESHIE FOGARTY

I had heard the phrase 'The Caseys of Sneem' since I was a young lad growing up on the side of Lower New Street in my hometown of Killarney. The name has reverberated down through the decades. Expressions such as 'the greatest', 'the strongest', 'the best in the world', 'sporting giants', 'the toughest' and much more capture the imaginations of generations of Kerry people whenever the name comes up for discussion. As a youngster in the 1940s and 1950s in Kerry the Caseys of Sneem influenced my thinking and that of any youthful sports person with ambitions of greatness in their own right and yet, despite all the praise and adulation showered on the name, not alone in Kerry but in England and America, the story of this remarkable family has never been told – until now.

The list of Casey sporting achievements are far too many to list here: Paddy was undefeated light and heavyweight wrestling champion of Ireland and his son, Patrick, was a member of the Vesta Rowing Club in London and won a medal in 1981 in the Henley Regatta; Paddy also won many long-distance cycling races in Ireland; Dan was a contractor, champion oarsman, and tug-of-war champion; Jack Casey had remained in Ireland, married and had taken up farming and fishing. He built the finest seine boats ever seen in the area. A superb oarsman in his own right, he helped win the

Salter Cup with his brothers and has ensured a family legacy of greatness – his son, Noel, grandchildren, Bernie and Caroline, and great-grandchildren, Jack and Victoria, are deeply involved in sports including, of course, rowing! Tom became British amateur boxing champion in 1937 after only nine days' training; Jim won the Canadian and South American wrestling titles; Mick, in a career that lasted over twenty years, had 200 wrestling bouts; and, of course, probably the greatest of them all, Steve retired undefeated as world wrestling champion. Most astounding of all was their non-participation in the Berlin Olympics of 1936 when they were barred from rowing there following their victory in the English rowing championships. The brothers were also unbeatable in tug-of-war, winning many titles. This amazing story of the Casey brothers is surely one of the most remarkable and inspiring of all. They left their native place, went forth and matched their prowess against the greatest sportsmen throughout the world. They earned undying fame and it can be said, without fear of contradiction, that this family of seven boys was 'the greatest of all'.

Christy Riordan lives in the town of Caherciveen deep in the heart of the Iveragh peninsula in County Kerry. He runs his own highly successful C/R video company together with his son Anthony and has been obsessed with the story of the Caseys all his life. He has been amassing the history of the family for decades but one aspect of this astonishing story had always eluded him. That was the narrative of the boys when emigration took them to America. Christy knew that the real source of information needed to complete his account of the Caseys family lay in Houston, Texas, where Jim Casey lived and died. Luck was on his side. When Jim's American-born wife, Myrtle, came to Sneem on holidays,

Christy Riordan pictured in Jim Casey's home in Dickinson, Texas, in April 2008 as he collected Casey family memorabilia for the book and DVD, *(l–r)*: Jim Hudson, his wife Mary and Myrtle Casey, Jim's wife Christy. The cup is the Governor's Cup, won by Tom Casey on the Charles River, Boston, in 1940 and presented by the Governor of Massachusetts, Leverett Saltonstall.

she was put in touch with Christy and, at her invitation Christy and I jetted out to Houston in February 2008 where we spent a wonderful week at Myrtle's home.

It was unforgettable seven days and we were given full access to the vast amount of memorabilia about the family that Myrtle has collected through the years – huge scrapbooks packed with priceless stories and information, stunning black-and-white photographs, audio interviews and even film footage of the boys competing in rowing and wrestling. We were introduced to Jim Hudson, the author of this book written in cooperation with Jim. Myrtle and Jim had sought out Hudson, mainly due to the fact that he had previously written *Dickinson – Taller than the Pines*, a superb history about their home place of Dickinson, Texas, published in 1979.

Dickinson, home to the Caseys, is on State Highway 3 at the edge of the Galveston metropolitan area in the northwest corner of Galveston County. Hudson explained how he was stunned as he listened to Jim recalling the family history and he was dumbfounded that their story had not received international recognition. A further fascinating insight into Jim Casey's fame as a sports personality and high standing in his community in Texas was vividly brought to us when we were introduced to and interviewed George Abbey, Director of Johnson Space Center (1996–2001).

He had served as an integral part of the NASA Shuttle-Mir Program, providing crucial oversight, management and guidance for the first phase of the International Space Station. He explained to us how Jim Casey had been approached by NASA to train many of the astronauts as they prepared for their flights into space. Further interviews were conducted by us with Myrtle and her daughter and the story, seemingly forgotten forever, was finally been pieced together. On our last night in Dickinson, Myrtle presented us with a copy of the original book written by Jim Hudson with Jim Casey and her written permission to have the book published

3038 Hughes Rd.
Dickinson, Texas 77539
U.S.A.
April 30, 2008

To whom it may concern:
 I have extended my permission for any and all photos, videos, news articles,
C D's and DVD to be used in preserving the story of the Casey family to Christy
Riordan and Weeshie Fogarty.
If they see fit to update the book written for Jim and Myrtle Casey, by Jim
Hudson, "The Toughest Family on Earth" , I give my permission to do so.
On a recent trip to Texas they suggested that the book be republished in Ireland
and the photos, etc. that they copied be added to complete the story of the Casey
family. A suggestion was made to rename the book and I agreed to that.
The people of Ireland want to read about this famous family and I agree to that.
I feel confident that these two men are sincere in their desire to see that the Casey
name will never die.

Myrtle Casey

Myrtle Casey
May 1, 2008

in Ireland. She was adamant that the story of the family
would finally be told to the world.

We flew home to Kerry determined to have this book
made available to sports lovers everywhere and now, thanks
to The Collins Press of Cork, Myrtle Casey's dream has come
true. Christy Riordan, however, has gone one step further
and a marvelous DVD chronicling the life and times of this
extraordinarily family from Sneem in County Kerry will also

be available – now people can listen to interviews with the family, view footage of their greatest victories and look at that collection of priceless memorabilia obtained on that unforgettable trip to Texas. However, for both Christy and myself, just one more journey needed to be made to complete the real story of the family.

The Casey family was born and raised in a tiny hamlet that sits upon the shore of the *Sneem River*. In May 2013, Christy and I, accompanied by our sons Anthony and Kieran, were rowed by local boatman Noel Donnelly to the old home, which now lies in ruins. It was a poignant and uplifting experience, more of a pilgrimage than a journey as we stood in silence at the very spot where this exemplary family had lived. Our journey, which had brought us to Houston, Texas, and all over Ireland, was complete and in that place it felt as if the spirits of the seven Casey brothers were reaching out. The story of the legendary Casey brothers is, without argument, one of the world's greatest sports stories. This book and DVD will fortify their place in history's pages.

INTRODUCTION

This is the story of an incredible Irish family. In particular, it details the amazing athletic feats of the seven brothers in that family, the Casey brothers of County Kerry. Nowhere in the annals of sport will you find an entire family so gifted: seven brothers uniquely equipped to star as Olympic-class oarsmen, tug-of-war champions, professional wrestlers and boxers. When you have read their story, you will undoubtedly agree that, if they weren't the 'toughest family on earth', they surely never found one that could beat them – at anything.

Let me be quick to point out that every word of this story is true. It is founded on fact, facts that have been documented in many places: in Ireland, England and the United States.

In their time, the athletic achievements of the Casey brothers won them a measure of fame throughout the sporting world. Today, they are still recognised as national heroes in their native Ireland, although some of their accomplishments took place over half a century ago. If they had had available to them then the worldwide sports coverage that is provided by the media today, they would surely be famous the word over. And if they had won four or five of the 1936 Olympic rowing events (as they should have), their names would be household words today.

Though late in the telling, this book attempts to win for the fabulous Casey brothers some measure of fame or, at least, some acknowledgment. Read on, then and see if you don't agree that the Casey brothers were, and perhaps still are, legendary.

JIM HUDSON

ONE

BEGINNINGS

In County Kerry, a tiny hamlet consisting of five houses sits upon the shore of the River Sneem. Named Ballaugh, it is situated near the coastal flatlands, which gradually rise into upland slopes and gentle hills that approach 2,000 feet in height. The nearest habitation of any consequence is the town of Sneem. No roads connect Ballaugh and Sneem; to go from one to the other, one must either trek overland through the hills for 4 miles or row a boat up the River Sneem for some 2 miles.

The inhabitants made, and still make, their living by fishing and farming. Fish can be sold in the local markets and restaurants in Sneem with any excess amounts exported from there. Farming is done mostly for home consumption; families in this area were and are more or less self-sustaining.

In the late 1800s the forebears of the Casey brothers lived in Ballaugh. Strangely enough, however, the two who were to bring the Casey brothers into the world never met until each had returned to Ireland from a stay in the United States.

Michael ('Big Mick') Casey was born in May 1877. Though not gigantic in size, he was enormously strong and a natural athlete. Both in Ireland and in America he was known as a 'brawler', a naturally tough and durable man who delighted in taking on all comers in fisticuffs or in wrestling.

3

Michael 'Big Mick' Casey was a naturally tough man who passed on his strength – of body and character – to his children.

This tag of 'brawler' was not nearly as disreputable then as it may sound today. As a matter of fact, it was then often used in a flattering way and the man so named was proud. In those days, organised and supervised athletic pursuits such as are commonly available today were lacking and men were oftentimes disposed to work off excess energy and fill their idle hours by engaging in impromptu fist fights or wrestling matches.

It is not known exactly when Mick Casey left for the United States but it must have been just before or at the turn of the century, when he was about twenty-three years old. He worked in the coal mines in Montana for a time before heading east and settling for a time in Boston, where he worked as stevedore loading and unloading freight for the Fall River Shipping Company. This line of work no doubt contributed even more to his strength and conditioning.

Still a 'brawler', he came to the notice of the great John L. Sullivan, who had been the world heavyweight bare-knuckle boxing champion. John L. took Big Mick into his camp for a time as his sparring partner. This fact alone is sufficient testimony to Big Mick's strength and skill. And what better triumph for a man who fancied himself a 'brawler' than to be asked to spar with the great John L. Sullivan.

In the same period, Big Mick was given the opportunity to wrestle with the heavyweight-wrestling champion 'Farmer' Burns who was reputed to have been one of the greatest wrestlers of all time. Years later, when his sons would press him for details about his bouts with John L. Sullivan or his match with 'Farmer' Burns, Big Mick would say only that each man, in his own way, had been 'a holy terror'. He never elaborated on how he had fared with them. He was probably a bit of a 'holy terror' himself, for both Sullivan and Burns.

During this same period, a young lady named Bridget Sullivan was living and working in Cambridge, Massachusetts. She was from County Kerry too but had gone off to America at about the same time as Mick Casey. Back in County Kerry, her family was held in high esteem because of their great strength and athletic skill. Bridget's two brothers, Dan 'Graffa Mountain' Sullivan and Patsy Sullivan, were fabled for their physical prowess and, it would seem, with ample justification.

There is the story still gleefully told about Dan Sullivan in County Kerry, although it undoubtedly dates from the 1800s. This was the time when Dan 'Graffa Mountain' Sullivan took on the British Navy – and won. It seems that part of the British fleet was anchored off the coast of Sneem and one evening they put ashore two boatloads of sailors in search of fresh food – in particular, fowl to supplement the meagre rations in their mess. Once ashore, they began rounding up and capturing chickens, geese and turkeys, causing a great commotion. The sailors intended to pay for the fowl they collected but Dan Sullivan, angrily observing the audacity of the sailors, either didn't know that or didn't believe it. With a bellow of rage, he flew out of his father's house and began to flatten sailors left and right. After he had knocked five or six of the sailors unconscious, his father ran out to stop him. The ten or twelve remaining sailors (most of whom, in those days, were Irish) were vastly relieved by Johnny 'Mountain' Sullivan's interference. If he hadn't stopped him, they swore Dan Sullivan would have flattened them all.

The next day, the British fleet commander, accompanied by three staff officers and three of the crewmen who had been involved in the ruckus, came ashore to apologise. Looking with a bemused grin at his three battered and bloodied crewmen and then at the 6-foot-225-pound Dan Sullivan, the admiral said that he had come not only to apologise but to get a good look at this rugged Irishman who had 'whipped the British Navy'.

The admiral would have marvelled to know that, for all of Dan 'Graffa Mountain' Sullivan's toughness, his father, Johnny 'Mountain' Sullivan, was generally acknowledged to be even tougher. Later on, when Bridget Sullivan wed Big

'Big Mick' Casey,
the scion of the
Casey clan, shown
in his later years.

Mick Casey, there was considerable rivalry between Mick and his fabled father-in-law.

Patsy Sullivan came to America with his sister Bridget, while Dan remained in Ireland where he did quite well for himself at farming and even better at rowing. He was generally acknowledged to be one of Ireland's finest oarsmen of that time. Bridget worked as a maid for a family in Cambridge, while her brother Patsy worked for the wealthy Vanderbilt family in Newport, Rhode Island. Later, Bridget joined Patsy in Newport and worked as a maid in the Vanderbilt home.

Eventually, Patsy Sullivan was placed in charge of navigation for the extensive fleet of yachts owned by the Vanderbilt family. Commodore Vanderbilt, who owned a fleet of Yankee Clipper sailing vessels engaged in the trans-Atlantic trade, had amassed the enormous Vanderbilt fortune. He was also a leading Wall Street financier and one of the so-called 'robber barons' that made millions in railroad stock transactions. He and his family had, for several years, financed American entries in the America's Cup yacht races, which America won consistently, year after year. Their principal competitor in the late 1800s was Scotland's Sir Thomas Lipton, founder of the Lipton tea empire. Though he financed no fewer than five entries in the America's Cup race between 1899 and 1930 (all of them named *Shamrock*), Sir Thomas was never able to beat the Vanderbilts who, like so many other wealthy residents of the Atlantic seaboard, were interested in all aspects of nautical competition. This applied to the racing of boats of all kinds, with and without sails.

For five or six weeks each year, the Newport–Rhode Island Regatta was held, pitting teams of oarsmen against one another in elimination matches until just one team emerged victorious. The boats were called 'double-bankers' – they were not unlike the classic boats called 'Boston Whalers'. There were six oars, three to each side in a staggered configuration. Each oar required two oarsmen pulling in tandem, resulting in a complement of twelve oarsmen, with a coxswain to set the pace.

The Vanderbilt traditionally competed in the regatta and their fierce desire to win this competition, as in the America's Cup challenges, caused them to spare no expense or effort in fielding a winning team. Sir Thomas Lipton fielded a team in Newport each year as well – this may have provided even more motivation for the Vanderbilts.

In the late 1890s, Patsy Sullivan approached the Vanderbilts with the suggestion that he should put together a rowing team for them – a team that he swore would beat anyone in the country or any foreign team as well. When he told them that some of the oarsmen he had in mind were back in Ireland, the Vanderbilts told Patsy that they would pay for their round-trip passage to America and their living expenses while in the country, if that would guarantee them a winning crew. So Patsy sent word back to Ireland for several cousins of his to come to America. Two were named Brennan (one of them named Mike), two were Burns and another was Sullivan, and they all came from Sneem.

To round out the crew, Patsy Sullivan sent word to Boston where there lived another strapping Irishman who had earned a reputation as a superb oarsman back home in Sneem. He was, of course, Big Mick Casey.

This racing crew, called 'The Hibernians', entered the Newport Regatta with a vengeance. For three years in a row, they remained unbeaten. Their crew was so strong that they made other champion-calibre crews look weak by comparison. Sir Thomas Lipton no doubt felt the same kind of frustration as he had in his America's Cup challenges, as The Hibernians from Sneem, overwhelmed his rowing team each year. It was ironic that this team of Irishmen rowing for an American family continued to beat one of the British Empire's wealthiest men and one of its outstanding sportsmen.

Some might think it remarkable that Bridget Sullivan and Big Mick Casey never met during these years in America. After all, they were both in Newport and both were working for the Vanderbilts but Mick was there only for the racing season – he spent five or six weeks there each year and after the season he returned to Boston. The principal deterrent to their meeting was surely the ironclad caste system that ruled society in those days. The wealthy east coast 'Brahmins' were extremely class-conscious, perhaps even more so than the British landed gentry whom they tried so hard to emulate. The idea that Mick Casey would ever enter the grounds of the Vanderbilt estate was unthinkable. To suppose that Bridget Sullivan would ever be invited by the Vanderbilts to view a regatta, even though their crew was composed of her countrymen, was equally unthinkable. In those bygone days, people knew their places and stayed firmly in them. So Bridget Sullivan would have stayed where she was, serving the Vanderbilts in their palatial home, which was patterned after the palace of the French 'Sun King', Louis XIV. It is possible that Bridget might have heard some word from her brother Patsy regarding this hard-muscled, hard-headed Mick Casey who was helping the Vanderbilt crew to win and she might have had born in her a spark of interest which was

Bridget Sullivan Casey, the heart of the Casey family.

to culminate in their eventual union, back home in Ireland. We shall never know.

This Bridget Sullivan, though not nearly as tall or as physically powerful as her two 'Mountain' brothers, had nonetheless benefited from the same genetic pool. She was a big-boned, strapping woman of remarkable strength and

The Casey family in the 1930s: *back row (l–r)*: Steve, Paddy, Jim, Mick, Jack and Dan. Tom was absent when this photo was taken; *front row (l–r)*: Kitty, Josephine (Jack's son Noel is on her knee), Bridget, Margaret and 'Big Mick'.

endurance and had the grace and physical bearing of a natural-born athlete. When we examine the careers of her seven sons later on in this book, it would be well to remember her contribution and that of her family to the combined genetic pool that produced them. The Sullivans were fabled athletes and men of great physical prowess. Some may think it remarkable that all seven Casey boys became outstanding athletes. When we take into account the infusion of Sullivan genes with those of the Caseys, we might speculate that, had she borne twice as many sons, all fourteen would likely have been remarkably strong. We might speculate, too, on what the outcome might have been and whether this story would be nearly as dramatic if Big Mick Casey had married anyone other than Bridget Sullivan. Surely, one would think, Big Mick's heritage would be enough to produce two or three or four strapping, athletic and unusually strong sons – but seven? No, not from a union with anyone but Bridget Sullivan, who was nearly as strong and as rugged as her fabled father and prodigious brothers.

As we shall see, her own physical attributes would be called upon and would serve her in good stead when, just a few years later, she was to bear and rear for Big Mick Casey a total of ten strapping children in just over thirteen years. That was after she and Mick Casey, at about the same time, returned to their native County Kerry. The union of these two – Big Mick Casey, the incredibly strong and agile 'brawler', boxer, wrestler and oarsman and Bridget Sullivan, feminine counterpart of the 'Mountain' Sullivans – was to be the stuff of which legends are made.

TWO

THE FORMATIVE YEARS

Mick and Bridget Casey settled into married life in a house built by Bridget's father. Later, with the help of their sons, they built a larger house nearby.

Soon after their marriage, in true Irish-Catholic tradition, the children came – and came – and came: Steve was born in December 1908; Paddy in February 1910; Jack in January 1911; Jim in February 1912; Mick in May 1913; Tom in July 1914; Mary Margaret in March 1916; Dan in June 1917; Josephine in April 1920; and, finally, Catherine in January 1922. And there was never a doctor in attendance for any of Bridget Casey's ten deliveries – a local midwife provided all the help she could get or needed.

What was life like for them in this out-of-the-way corner of the world in the early part of the twentieth century? It certainly wasn't easy. Their dirt-floored home had three bedrooms on the second floor and one bedroom downstairs. Privacy must have been at a premium to say the least. The remainder of the ground floor was given over to one large open room with a huge open-hearth fireplace. This large room served as living room, kitchen and dining room (and there were, no doubt, some little bodies sprawled on blankets here and there when bedtime came). Meals were cooked in pots over the fireplace, which was the only source of heat in the house and which burned turf that Mick and the boys cut from the nearby bogs. There was no electricity and illumination was provided by kerosene lamps. There was no plumbing either. Water for drinking, cooking, bathing and laundry had to be drawn from the river. During dry spells, the water had to be drawn from natural springs, a trek of about a mile and a half each way, loaded down with heavy galvanised pails full of water on the return trip. An out-house sat at the rear of the property but the boys were inclined to answer the call of nature wherever they might find themselves in this lonely space nearly empty of any people other than themselves.

The Casey land holding extended a distance of about 3 miles back from the water's edge and was about 2 miles in width. The land rose slowly from the coastline and rose into the hills and mountains, some 2,000 feet in height. Four or five acres of the flat bottomland were given over to cultivation: cabbage, turnips, onions, the ubiquitous potato and other garden crops. Chickens, turkeys, ducks and geese were kept on the land; the indomitable Bridge Casey fed and watered them daily and she and the girls collected their eggs.

On Mick Casey's father's farm, located some 8 miles away, Mick kept fifteen to twenty milk cows and Bridget and the girls milked those that were fresh twice each day.

Up to 250 sheep were kept up in the hills, marked on their sides in red paint with the letters 'M C' (for Mick Casey). The boys were detailed to help the dogs in herding the sheep to keep them from straying too far afield. They also learned very early, at five or six years of age, to help with the foaling of lambs in the springtime. The nickname for kids living in those hills was 'Kerry goats' – the boys constantly ran up and down those hills in pursuit of their animals or just in exuberant play. They raced one another all the time. In fact, in everything they did, they competed. Even when doing their chores, such as digging turf from the bog, turning over the garden for their mother or picking cabbages, they raced against each other. They were born with fiercely competitive natures, most probably inherited from Big Mick.

Later, when physical conditioning become critical to their success in rowing competitions, they would run up and down these 2,000-foot hills again and again, racing each other as they worked out. One can easily imagine that even when they were disciplining and training their bodies, these boys were still just having fun.

Their father, Mick, was a good provider and their mother, Bridget, a good cook who saw to it that they were never hungry. Their ordinary fare, while simple, was ample. Corned beef, potatoes and cabbage and carrots – all boiled together – were common dishes. When the boys were in serious training for their boat races, Bridget arranged for Old Man 'Batt' Burns, the only butcher in Sneem, to deliver special cuts of meat (steaks, chops and roasts) to the house. It is interesting to note that the meat was delivered by the local postman, Steve 'Batt' Burns, the butcher's son. He cycled all over the peninsula on his postal route, something that prepared him well for later cycling races in which he won the Irish national championship. He was helped in his pursuit by one of the incredible Casey brothers, as we shall see later on in their story. Steve 'Batt' Burns' brother, Paddy, was also a great track and field athlete.

At any rate, Bridget Sullivan Casey fed her athlete sons well. When they were in training, a typical breakfast consisted of eggs, bacon, ham, black pudding, homemade bread (either 'heavy' bread or raisin bread) and lots of buttermilk. When her 'Kerry goats' returned from their training runs, up the hills, down the other side and all the way back – a distance of some 4 miles (and all done in bare feet) – she had a substantial meal waiting for them, highlighting those special cuts of meat from Mr Burns' butcher shop. The small game the boys brought home from hunting forays – rabbit, hare, or squirrel – found their way into the stew pot as well. Every night when they came home for bed, they found a pot of porridge by the fireplace (a little something to tide them over until morning), left by their mother. There was fresh or smoked fish every day, most often salmon, fresh-caught in the nearby waters.

The method of fishing that Mick Casey employed was common to that part of the world: he ran out two or three trotlines, each a half-mile long, across the estuary. Tied every few feet along these long lines was a three-foot line with a baited hook. Twice a day, each morning and evening, the boys rowed out along these trotlines removing fish and re-baiting hooks. There were also some dozen lobster pots or traps, which had to be pulled up, examined and emptied of their catch every morning and every evening. The boys rowed for miles each day, four at the oars and one steering. Their first exposure to rowing came as an important part of their work ethic, under the stern eye and the crisp instructions of their impatient and demanding father. As if this wasn't enough rowing for them, they would rush to the boat and try to race any boatman who happened along their stretch of the river. This early basic training was to prove invaluable just a short while later when they became serious oarsmen in local competitions.

But until they got a little older, they had to be content to wait and watch and learn as their father competed as part of a local team in races held on Waterville Lake. Mick was part of a four-man crew in a type of racing boat called 'Four-oar Sweeps'. There were two oars to a side, staggered, one man to an oar and with stationary (rather than sliding) seats. Besides Mick, there were two O'Connor brothers and Jack Sullivan (no relation to Bridget). Their coxswain was seventy-year-old Paddy 'Shine' Connor.

The boys were accustomed to running several miles cross-country through the mountains after their father left to compete in a race, concealing themselves atop a small hill which overlooked the lake so that they could observe the races without their father's knowledge. He always denied them permission to go and watch, for reasons of his own. It may be that he could not bear to have his sons watch him lose, which he sometimes did, although that did not happen often. But there were the Mahoneys from Ardcost in County Kerry whom his crew could never beat. Then there was the 'Whiddy Crew': this was a group of fishermen from Whiddy Island in Bantry Bay, County Cork. Not only did Mick's crew never beat the Whiddy Crew but the crew had never been beaten by anyone else in those days.

So the boys watched and waited and learned and hoped, as they watched their father and his crew rowing. They took special note of the Mahoneys and the Whiddy Crew and, no doubt, daydreamed of the day when they would avenge their father's defeats at their hands.

While on the subject of rowing – picture this if you will: the closest school was in the town of Sneem. Each morning, after rising at five o'clock and frantically washing, dressing, eating and running the trotlines and checking the lobster pots, the boys made a mad dash up the river into Sneem. From their landfall near the town, it was another mile and a

Ruins of the Casey home in Sneem, County Kerry, where 'Big Mick' and Bridget Casey reared ten children. As the family got older they built another bigger house not far from this old stone residence. Photograph courtesy Anthony Riordan.

half to the school. The children ran that distance each morning but were invariably late for their first classes. The school administrators, knowing their circumstances, made allowances for them and never disciplined them for it. Meanwhile, their good mother, Bridget, rowed the boat back to Ballaugh and returned in mid-afternoon to pick up the children for the ride back home. It was a rushed trip home to get all the evening chores underway.

The boys often went off with the family dogs to do a little hunting. Taking advantage of Big Mick's occasional absences, they would 'borrow' his antiquated shotgun, a single barrelled piece with which they hunted otter, badger, fox and other small animals whose pelts could be sold. Each time they fired the old gun, the barrel would fall off and the gun had to be reassembled before the next shot. Little did they know then that several of them would, when grown, have the opportunity and the financial wherewithal to hunt exotic big game in several countries and on different continents. Big Mick could not have been unaware of the 'borrowing' of his old shotgun and shells but he never chastised the boys too severely. He knew not only that 'boys will be boys' but he was also wise enough to know that soon these boys would be men and small game hunting was one of the traditional rites of passage.

The boys' favourite pastime of all was 'scuffling'. Had you seen them at it late in the evening, grappling, pushing, shoving, kicking, throwing one another to the ground, you would have called it wrestling but they did not. They, and everyone else in County Kerry, called it 'scuffling'. How they loved it. It stayed light a good part of the year until quite late at night – sometimes as late as eleven o'clock and many was the time when Bridget Casey had to threaten them with the wrath of their father or Big Mick himself had to threaten, in order to get them to stop their 'scuffling' and go in to their beds. Of course, Mick knew a few things about wrestling. He could not have stayed with great 'Farmer' Burns back in his brawling days if he had not. So he showed the boys a few basic holds but really didn't give them too much in the way of encouragement. They knew that the basic premise of wrestling was that to win a match, you had to pin your opponent's two shoulders to the ground for a count of three seconds. So they went at it for hours – brother against brother – grappling, sprawling, clutching and throwing one another in the tall grass. (Mick's only complaint about their 'scuffling' was that they were matting down the grass so badly that the cows couldn't eat it.) Whenever he complained, they would move their bouts to a fresh, untrampled arena. They were rough and tough these Casey boys, young 'brawlers' cast in their father's mould and having their mother's added measures of strength and endurance thrown in. Their 'scuffling' was rough and earnest. There were bloodied noses, torn ligaments and probably some mild concussions given and received in these frequent free-for-alls. The Coffey boys and the Mahoney boys who lived nearby joined in the scuffling just once or twice and then elected to find playmates elsewhere. So the Casey boys continued to fight each other, each one striving to gain superiority over the other, whether younger or older.

So it was that in their daily rowing and in their constant scuffling, they were learning and growing day by day in the skills that were to bring them renown in the not-too-distant future.

Fame and fortune were not far from their minds as they rowed and fought, ran and jumped, played at tug-of-war and, in many healthy ways, began to develop into the strapping, incredibly strong athletes that they were on the verge of becoming. None of them actively pursued fame; it came to them almost naturally as a consequence of their healthy bodies, hard work and the belief that no Casey could be beaten at anything, so long as there was the breath of life left in him.

The challenges to the Casey clan lay not too far ahead.

THREE

SIGNS OF GREATNESS

While still in their early teens, the Casey brothers began to compete in the 'Junior' boat races held in County Kerry. From the beginning to the end of these competitions, they were never beaten.

Steve, Paddy, Jack and Jim manned the oars while younger brother Tom served as coxswain. They had about them, even then, a natural grace of style, a kinship of spirit that made them row as one, each boy seemingly interlocked with the others as they swept the oars alongside the boat. On shore, they might compete with each other fiercely, all day long, but once in the boat, they became a team of one mind.

At the end of each sweep through the water, they raised their oars in perfect unison, twisting the oars to turn the glistening blade edges cleanly into the water, cutting through the resisting surface with no visible or apparent effort. The powerful shoulders and arms sent the boat swiftly and smoothly down the course, seeming to skim along the water's surface rather than dragging through it.

They sat upright in their rowing positions. As they stretched out their arms to position the oars for the next downward stroke, they remained nearly upright, not bending or lurching forward as did the crews of other boats. They were tireless. They could row for miles just to get to the site of a race and then take on all comers all day long and beat them – and beat them they did. They were never beaten as 'Juniors'.

When he was about fifteen, Steve Casey, the oldest boy, began rowing with his father's crew, replacing Jack Sullivan. With this combination – the two O'Connors, Big Mick and Steve, with old Paddy 'Shine' Connor still at cox – they began winning more races than had the old crew.

But they still could not win a race against the Mahoneys or against the Whiddy Crew. A year or so later, Big Mick gave up his seat in the boat to his son Paddy. The team won even more races with this infusion of younger blood and muscle but the Mahoneys still beat them, much to Big Mick's consternation.

At this point, the boys thought that, having consistently won in all their Junior class competitions, they were ready to take their place alongside boats crewed by men, not boys. Oddly enough, they received no encouragement from their father in realising this goal. The boys didn't know why he seemed to want to hold them back. He used to stand on shore and time them as they rowed over a measure course but he would never tell them their time or how well or how poorly he thought they had done. Of course, they had no watch of their own to check their time. At any rate, Big Mick seemed to be biding his time and to want them to do the same. One must remember that youth is impetuous and also that Caseys are competitive, to put it mildly.

When they got no encouragement from their father, the boys took matters into their own hands. They plotted, in an elaborate scheme, to enter a boat race in Cahersiveen – a town located on the other side of the peninsula.

They secretly arranged to borrow a boat from a boat builder named Murphy, whose boat yard lay across the bay. In their father's absence, the boys rowed 10 miles across the bay and secured the racing gig behind their boat with ropes. That night, under cover of darkness, they towed the boat back across the 10 miles of water to a dock at Sneem, where they placed the racing boat on the back of a borrowed truck. To ensure their secrecy, the truck was hidden out of sight until the following morning.

Rising very early, the young conspirators met with the truck and drove to the site of the regatta in Cahersiveen; five big, strapping bodies crammed into the bed of the truck with the hulk of the racing gig suspended above them.

When they arrived at the course, they put their boat into the water, took their positions at the oars and began rowing the four-mile course so as to become familiar with it. While doing so, they looked over the crews in the other boats to get a feel for their competition. Their hearts began to beat a little faster when they realised that the Mahoneys were there.

Meanwhile, back at Ballaugh, Mick Casey could not help noticing that his five oldest sons were nowhere to be seen. The boys had, of course, taken their mother in on their secret so that she would not be needlessly worried. She kept their secret from Big Mick as long as she could. Finally, his persistent bellowing was more than she could stand and she was forced to tell him of their secret venture into the world of adult racing competition.

Big Mick Casey was furious. His boys had taken it upon themselves to do something, in secret, that Big Mick had told them they could not do. He set out for Cahersiveen in a towering rage.

Even as the time for the start of the race drew closer, the Casey boys continued to row the boat around the course, getting familiar with it and eyeing the men in the other boats – men against whom they were soon to compete. There were some fine physical specimens in those boats: large, strong men who seemed to exert little effort as they stroked their oars. The sight of them might have struck fear into the hearts of the Casey boys, especially since the Mahoneys were among them, but they did not. The sight of them simply brought home to the boys the fact that they would have to row their strongest race if they were to have any hope of beating these men and they quietly encouraged each other to do just that.

As they began rowing toward the starting line, marked by a string of buoys floating on the water, they heard a voice bellowing from far off. The boys looked up to see a committee boat approaching them at some distance, a figure towering in front of the boat screaming and waving. They recognised the voice before they could make out the man's features. It was a voice they knew well enough: Big Mick Casey's.

'What are you doing here? What do you think you're about? Who told you you could do this? By God, I'll teach you a lesson you'll never forget. Row that boat over there and keep rowing until I tell you to stop.' He was gesturing to the part of the river behind the starting line where, by now, all the other boats had begun to line up for the start of the race.

Every fearful of their father's wrath, the boys did as they were told and rowed the boat past and beyond the starting line. When they had gone a quarter of a mile, Big Mick shouted, 'All right, turn around.' And as the boys turned the boat back in the direction of the starting line, Mick screamed to the starter, 'Fire the gun, fire the gun, start the race now,' before reluctantly agreeing to pleas to allow the boys to come to the starting line.

So, as the boys drew abreast of the other boats, the starter fired his gun and they were away – these young lads racing powerful, experienced adult oarsmen. They tried to put out of their minds the fact that their own father had tried to penalise them – punish them – by imposing a quarter-mile handicap upon them. They gave up trying to understand why. Instead, they gritted their teeth and dug their oars into the water, grimly stroking in perfect unison, their minds devoted only to the challenge of the race before them.

They had not got off to a good start, having been rattled by their father's ranting and had to stroke at a furious pace to keep from falling hopelessly behind.

The distance between them and the last boat seemed never to decrease but slowly and steadily they overtook and, finally, passed it. This gave them new hope and an added measure of determination to see the race through.

Their boat seeming to glide upon the surface in an un-interrupted silken path, they moved past another labouring crew and then another and another. Finally, incredibly, with just a quarter of a mile remaining of the four-mile course, there was but one boat remaining ahead of them. That boat was crewed by the Mahoneys. Groaning, praying, softly urging each other on, they picked up their stroke until their arms were pumping like windmills and they dug harder and deeper into the yielding water, driving their arms and shoulders with all the strength their young bodies could bring to bear.

From the corners of their eyes, they saw the Mahoneys begin to slip slowly, slowly to the stern of their own boat. They saw the straining, grunting men desperately striving to keep up with them. Then, with the Mahoney boat far astern, the young Caseys streaked past the finish line. They had won the race by two boat lengths.

Legends are made of this sort of athletic feat – and a legend it soon became. It was repeated all over County Kerry and even further still. Five teenage boys in their first adult competition had beaten some of the finest crews of grown men and had beaten them handily. And this was in spite of their father's unsettling interference and obvious rage.

What was their father's reaction to all this? Well, to say he was proud doesn't quite convey how he felt. He was filled to bursting with fatherly pride – that much was obvious. But still, he didn't make too much over the boys. He simply murmured, 'You did well; you did fine,' as he patted each on the back. By now, he and a number of other men were heading for a nearby pub. The boys busied themselves with lifting the boat out of the water and securing it onto the borrowed truck.

When they had finished, they too went up to the pub but being underage, they had to sip ginger ale in a small room apart from the main bar. They could see into the bar and could hear most of what was said there.

Mostly, they heard their father. Big Mick stood, with his pint in his hand, holding forth to an attentive crowd of local sportsmen and when the boys heard what he was saying, they began to understand a little of their father's behaviour over the past weeks and months. He was saying, 'I couldn't believe the time they made. They were faster than anybody ever was. They beat the best time that we were ever able to make – that included the Connors, all others and myself.'

Here was a clue to Big Mick's secrecy. If he was anything at all, Big Mick was a proud man. He was proud of his strength, agility and skill in rowing, and here were his children, his teenage boys, beating his best time. How his pride in them must have fought with his own wounded pride in himself. No wonder he could never bring himself to tell them what the frozen hands on his stopwatch had told him.

Then they heard their father saying, ' I tried to hold them back. You saw me. You heard me. I wanted them to have to start from behind the line so that I could teach them a lesson. Imagine them doing this without my permission.' Then, with a twinkle in his eye and a nudge in the ribs of the fellow nearest him, he went on, 'Besides, I didn't want them to win too big. Hell, if word got out about how good they are, what kind of bets d'you think I could get against them?'

The boys now knew that there was more to their father's ranting and raving than just their disobedience. He undoubtedly knew that they could win a race such as this but he had not been able to coach them beforehand about holding back so as not to win by too great a margin. If they won going away, who was he to find to bet against them in the future races? They began to understand too, why he had not divulged to them the time they had made racing against the clock. He wanted no one to know; if he didn't tell them, then they most surely could not let it slip to others.

For whatever devious reasons Big Mick had acted as he had, it was apparent that he had more than an inkling of what he had in these five boys of his – and with two more coming up behind.

His bragging in that pub robbed him of a chance for a grudge match and the prospect of some easy money from the Mahoneys. For, unseen by Big Mick, one of the Mahoneys, or one of their friends, overheard him and got the word out to them. They wanted nothing more to do with these young Casey brothers.

Big Mick spent a good deal of time in that pub, basking in the reflected glory of his boys' unbelievable win. While they sat unnoticed in the other room, Big Mick was revelling in the congratulations and accepting the praise of his cronies, and thinking of days to come and races to be won. Whether or not Big Mick knew before this legendary race just how good his boys really were, he had absolutely no doubts now. He knew, as did everyone who had seen that race, that the Casey boys were winners but he could not know, and nor could they, that this was just the start of the winning – boat-racing was only one of the sports in which they would compete and would consistently win.

FOUR

WINNING ... WINNING ... WINNING

After their incredible win at Cahersiveen, the Casey brothers entered race after race in towns and villages up and down the coast of Ireland. They won them all. Big Mick was there at all these events, laying bets on his boys with all who wished to do so and limiting his instructions to the lads to telling them not to win too handily.

'Now, you don't have to beat them badly; don't run away from them; just beat them by a half length or so. No need scarin' them all off now, is there?' he would say. Mick always had his eye on the next race and the next bet and he didn't want to scare off the competition on the one hand or end up with no one willing to cover his bets on the other. So, he cautioned them again and again – 'Hold back boys. You don't have to win too big – just win.'

After about a year, they boys finally had a chance to avenge their father's losses at the hands of the Whiddy Crew and in the Whiddys' own back yard, so to speak. A regatta was held in Bantry Bay, County Cork. With the exception of the Casey boys from County Kerry, all the other crews were local and were nothing if not proud and self-confident. The Whiddy Crew, being from Whiddy Island in the middle of Bantry Bay, could certainly be counted on to compete in this race, as indeed they did. They were all fishermen between the ages of thirty and thirty-five; strong, strapping, barrel-chested men who had won many a race and who were quite confident of winning this one.

The Casey boys were using a fine boat built by Pat O'Neill. They had borrowed it for this race but later they would buy it from Pat and use it again and again.

The Whiddy Crew were in a fine boat too, one built by Pat Kilderry, who was considered among the finest of the boat builders in all of County Cork.

The four boats in the race took off from the line in a fair start. The Whiddy Crew were rowing feverishly, determined not to be overtaken by this crew of young upstarts from Kerry. Try as they might, they could not pull away from these splendid young athletes who appeared to be rowing all out but were actually holding back from a maximum effort. They were following Mick's advice to the letter – God help them if they didn't – and were simply holding their position instead of making an all-out effort. They kept up this pretence until the finish line was but a quarter of a mile away. Then they intensified their efforts and left the Whiddy Crew in their boiling wake, winning the race by a boat length.

The men from Whiddy Island pulled in to shore and tied up along the left side of a long pier that jutted out into the bay, while the Casey boys tied up on the opposite side. The Whiddy Crew were furious. How could they, who had taken on and beaten nearly all comers, have been beaten by a crew of mere boys?

''Twas the boat,' they said. 'You have a better boat than ours. You'd never have beaten us if we had been in your boat and you in ours.'

Mick had counselled the boys not to say anything derogatory to the Whiddy Crew. He had instructed them to tell them that they had had to do their very best to beat them. 'Don't let on; tell 'em you really had to work hard,' he said.

So, when the Whiddy Crew blamed their boat for their defeat, Big Mick challenged them to race his boys again – this time exchanging boats so that the Whiddys were in the Caseys' boat and vice versa. However, this agreement was reached only after Big Mick insisted on doubling the size of his bet, seeing as how the Casey boys would now be staying the night in County Cork. At about one o'clock the following afternoon, the challenge match was held. The crews took their seats – each in their competitors' boat – and the race was on.

With the exception of the fact that only two boats were competing, rather than four, this race was a carbon copy of the one that had been raced the day before. Again the boys held back from mounting an all-out effort; again they won but this time by only half a boat length.

At last, they had had their revenge on the men from Bantry Bay who had so consistently beaten their father's crew. They had beaten them, not just once, but twice, and at the Whiddy's own insistence. How sweet it must have been for Big Mick to collect their wagers – doubled and in spades.

As sweet as this victory might have been, it was only a foretaste of the sweet winnings yet to be tasted.

FIVE

KILLARNEY

One of the most prestigious racing regattas held each year in Ireland is the Killarney Regatta. Its history dates to at least the 1830s although there may well have been races there even earlier than this.

Held on Lake Leane, near Innisfallen, County Kerry, a lovely area of rivers and lakes dotted with shimmering emerald islets – the regatta attracts competitors and spectators from all over Ireland and from many other countries as well.

The most prestigious event in the Killarney Regatta was the running of the open four-oar race for the Salter Challenge Cup. The Killarney racing committee had held on to this cup for many, many years and it would seem, based on the incredible rules they established for winning it, that they might hold on to it forever. To win the Salter Cup, a single crew had to win the open four-oar race not just once but three years in a row. Given that some of the finest oarsmen in the world were competing for this coveted cup each year, such a feat seemed to be beyond the realm of possibility for **any** crew.

The formidable Whiddy Crew won the event in 1925. In 1926, however, the Aghadoe Crew prevailed and the Whiddy

Crew apparently failed to be placed. (It may be that the Whiddy Crew did not enter in 1926. The semi-official history of Killarney, *Killarney's Rowing Story – Two Hundred Years of History*, published in 1986, contains no mention of the Whiddy Crew having participated in any race there in 1926. It would stand to reason, I would think, that if the Whiddy Crew had participated in the regatta in 1926, they would have been placed in at least one of the events. They were an excellent group of oarsmen, as the Casey brothers knew full well.)

For some unknown reason, the Killarney Regatta was not held in the years 1927, 1928 or 1929. When the races resumed in 1930, the Casey brothers, while still very young compared to the seasoned crews against whom they would have to compete, were eager to enter the open four-oar race and were confident that they would be able to bring that cherished silver trophy, the Salter Cup, to the Casey mantelpiece. That they would have to win this event three years running was, for them, a minor inconvenience rather than an overwhelming challenge. So, with Dan as coxswain, Steve at stroke and Paddy, Tom and Jim rounding out the crew, the Casey brothers won the open fours competition in 1930 and again in 1931.

In 1932, the Killarney Regatta was not held. At any rate, when racing resumed in 1933, the Caseys were told that they would not be given the Salter's Cup if they should win the four-oar race, since the rules read that the event must be won in three consecutive years. Since no race had been held in 1932, the committee maintained the Caseys would have to start again to put together a string of three consecutive victories. This was the first instance (but certainly not the last) of racing committees trying to 'stack the deck' against these upstart young men from Ballaugh.

One can only imagine Big Mick Casey's reaction to this transparent tactic that was meant only to deny the Caseys their rightful due if they were to win again. He flew into a rage and directed such a barrage of objections at the committee, including the threat of legal action, that they finally relented and agreed that, should the boys win again, the cup was theirs to take.

Firstly, of course, they had to win. Pitted against them on that lovely and memorable day of Sunday 6 August 1933 were some of the finest crews that Ireland had ever seen. They included crews from St Brendan's Rowing Club in Waterville, Kenmare, Castletownbere, Bere Island, the Mahoneys from Ardcost and last, but not least, the formidable oarsmen from Whiddy Island.

To qualify for the final Challenge Cup race, a series of preliminary heats were run. The Caseys won all of theirs to qualify. As fate would have it, the Whiddy Crew were beaten in the preliminaries and were eliminated from participation in the final heat.

The Casey boys really wanted to win the Salter Cup. They wanted to win it for their father, for their mother, for Sneem, Ballaugh and County Kerry. Most of all, they wanted to win it for themselves – for the Casey brothers. So, in this final championship race, they pulled out all the stops. There was no holding back here; no pretence at mighty effort while simply holding their own; they ran this race all out to win.

And win they did, by a good four lengths over a superb St Brendan's team, who finished second. So, in the history of the regatta cited above, it is said '... much to the lamentation

Four of the Caseys, (*l–r*) Dan, Steve, Tom, Jim, who won the Salter Challenge Cup in the four-oar sweeps – Paddy was also a member of that crew. To win the cup, they had to secure victories in three consecutive years – they did this with wins in 1930, 1931 and 1933.

of the Regatta Committee, the mighty men of Ballaugh triumphed and brought home the Salter Cup for good. It still rests at the Casey household in Ballaugh and is now valued at £1200.' Immediately after the race, the Regatta Committee offered to buy back the cup for £60 but, of course, the Caseys refused. That committee simply didn't want to give up that cup.

As another parenthetical note, I am happy to be able to report that, despite the fierce ongoing competition engaged in the Killarney Regatta and in many others, the Casey brothers became fast friends with the members of the

Whiddy Crew. There was mutual admiration between them, as both crews were seemingly possessed of superhuman drive and an overwhelming desire to win. The Caseys had a great deal of respect for the super athletes from Whiddy Island. Fifty years later, in 1983, five of the Casey brothers returned to Sneem in a nostalgic reunion. They were reunited with a couple of the members of the old Whiddy Crew and they all had a marvellous time recounting and reliving their exploits of a half century before.

The winning of the Salter Cup in 1933 ensured a prominent place in Irish sporting history, and in Irish legend as well, for the Casey brothers. However, for the Caseys, great as this triumph had been, there were far more cups, trophies, victories and championships to win. Not all of them were to be won in boat races, although there were surely many of these left to come.

1933 CASEYS TAKE SALTER TROPHY FOR THREE-IN-A-ROW

Killarney Regatta, held on Sunday 6th August 1933, was a big success as ever. Favoured by delightful weather, the Regatta, held on the Innisfallen course, had all the ingredients of Regattas of old. All vantage points on the lakeshore were thronged, especially Innisfallen Island, from which an admirable view of the course could be had. The races were as keen and exciting as one could wish for and spectators were satisfied with a great day's sport. The Killarney Pipers' Band rendered musical selections during the intervals between the races and these selections were appreciated by all. A quote from the 'Kerryman' of the time says: 'the Committee may well feel proud of their energetic efforts to revive this once famous regatta.'

The Committee in 1933 was as follows: Chairman Mr. T.M. O'Sullivan; Treasurers Major Phelps, Mr. A.J. McGillycuddy; Hon. Secretaries Mr. D.C. Counihan, Mr. A. Smyth; Committee; J. Murphy, J. Counihan, D. O'Connor, T. Hill, M. Horgan, C. O'Keefe, D.P. O'Sullivan, D. O'Brien, E. O'Sullivan, J. Moriarty, J. O'Shea, P. O'Connell, E. Cronin, P. Cronin, Sir Maurice O'Connell, M. Talbot, Dr. Whelan, D.R. O'Donoghue, J. Fleming.

DETAILS:
Junior Sixes for Flesk Valley Challenge Cup.
1st Heat: Workmen 1st; Commercials 2nd; Muckross 3rd. Won by three lengths with a bad third.

2nd Heat: Aghadoe 1st; Flesk Valley 2nd; Brendan's 3rd. Won by two lengths. Winning crew: J. Mannix, B. Egar, J. Rabh, J. Doyle, J. Purcell, J. Taylor (stroke) D. Hayes (Cox).
Juvenile Sixes for Lough Leane Challenge Cup. Aghadoe 1st; Commercials 2nd; Muckross 3rd. This was a great race. Commercials held a fairly good lead up to about 50 yards of the winning post when Aghadoe came with a great burst to win a most exciting finish by a length. Muckross were two lengths away in third. Winning crew: M. Griffin, P. Griffin, N. Courtney, M. Cronin, T. Foran, T. Courtney, D. Lynch (cox).
Ladies Sixes for Flesk Valley Challenge Cup. Muckross 1st; Flesk Valley 2nd.
Only two crews competed and Muckross won easily. Winning crew: Misses J. Hennessey, K. McLeod, L. Counihan, M. Tangney,

Mrs. P. Coffey, Miss A. Phelps (stroke), T. O'Shea (cox).

Senior Sixes Challenge Cup

Aghadoe were warm favourites for this event, and they justified this by winning a great race by half a length. Two lengths divided second and third. Winning crew: N. McGurn, J. Guerin, J. Sullivan, J. Sullivan, P. Courtney, G. Cronin (stroke), D. Lynch (cox).

Open Four-Oar Race for Salter Challenge Cup

Casey Brothers 1st; St. Brendan's 2nd. Won by four lengths. Winning crew: Messrs. Casey Bros., Sneem.

The McGillycuddy Perpetual Challenge Cup was won by Aghadoe who obtained the highest number of points.

The Salter Challenge Cup: The Caseys will keep it forever.

SIX

ALL SEVEN NOW

During the early 1930s, the boys were racing everywhere, in every race they could enter and in every configuration of boat: singles, doubles, four-oars, sixes, and were constantly winning.

Soon, the two youngest boys, Tom and Dan, were ready to take their places with the others. So Mick Casey now had a six-oar crew ready to take on all comers, with Dan, the youngest, to serve as coxswain. But Mick needed a boat fine enough to carry his winning crew. Finding none fine enough for him to buy, he contracted with Johnny Gallivan to build a boat for him. Johnny had a willing group of young lads to help: the Casey brothers, anxious to board and row this craft, pitched in and worked from dawn to dusk to expedite its completion.

To say that the boat was built from scratch is no exaggeration, for the boys went into the woods and felled the strongest oak trees they could find. From them, they planed 6-foot long strips, using cross-saws, always going with the grain, precisely one and one half inches wide and half an inch thick. These strips were placed in lengths of pipe and heated over a fire to allow them to be precisely curved before being securely attached to the hand-formed keel. They worked steadily for weeks, until finally they had produced a magnificent boat – perfectly balanced, crafted for minimum drag and sleekly curved.

With this fine boat, the Casey brothers went from regatta to regatta, emerging each time in triumph. By now, other crews were hesitant about racing them, even though they were still adhering to Big Mick's edict: 'Don't run away from 'em, just beat 'em.'

Big Mick also continued his practice of going off to the nearest pub with his cronies after each race, accepting their congratulations and buying them a few rounds with his winnings. The boys were left to fend for themselves and would have gone hungry on many occasions had it not been for the local womenfolk who took pity on them and fed them dinner. Those were acts of charity that must have taken off a few years in Purgatory – feeding seven strapping, starving Casey boys. The boys had no money of their own to speak of, so they could hardly have taken care of their needs on their own.

The Caseys' final encounter with the Whiddy Crew ended in an inglorious embarrassment for the fishermen from Bantry Bay. Word had got around about the Caseys' new boat and competition was becoming hard for them to find. So they entered a regatta in Castletown Berehaven in County Cork, away from the familiar landscape of County Kerry.

Three other boats had entered: a crew from Bere Island, another from Castletown and the Whiddy Crew. When the Caseys arrived at the scene, all three of these boats pulled out of the competition, refusing to race the Caseys in their new boat.

In disgust and frustration, the Caseys cast about for another boat to use in the race. The only boat available there was a weather-beaten working boat that had been sitting on stays, bottom up, for many months. It was so weathered that the boys had to get pieces of turf from a nearby bog and rub them down the bottom and sides of the boat. They then got handfuls of sticky black mud from the river bottom and slapped it on the boat's outer surfaces, in the hope of providing enough caulking to let them run the race without sinking first. The boat was equipped with 'clamp' type oarlocks, which restricted the lateral movement of the oars. However, it was all they could come up with and they were prepared to give it a try.

When they had done all that they could to revive this derelict boat, they rowed it out to the starting line under the watchful eye of the race committee. The committee members laughed at the size of this rounded hulk and jokingly referred to it as 'American Liner'.

The three other crews, seeing the Caseys struggling with this large, ungainly tub of a boat, were now willing to go to the starting line. With the crack of the starter's gun, the other three boats pulled quickly away, leaving the Caseys and their weather-beaten boat in their wakes.

The Casey boys pulled out all the stops. No holding back, no easing up, they rowed as they had never rowed before, except perhaps when they had been rowing against Big Mick's stopwatch.

The gunwales were high, making the angle of the oars very steep and awkward. The seats were old, weathered planks full of splinters. Water sloshed in the bottom of the boat, moving forward then backward as the boat lunged and then paused momentarily between sweeps of the oars.

Groaning, sweating, pulling, straining, the Casey boys rowed their hearts out. The course was 4 miles long; they did not catch the trailing boat until they had gone a mile and a half. To make matters even more difficult, they were rowing into a headwind for the first 2 miles. The high bow and raised sides of their old tub were affected far more by the wind than were the sleek, low boats of their competitors.

The boys told each other, 'If we can just hold our own until we make the turn, we'll have wind behind us. Then we can make a race of it.'

Still straining mightily, the boys made the turn. Sure enough, the wind that had been their enemy just moments before, became their ally, giving their boat a critical push as they skimmed over the water in pursuit of the other boats. Slowly, steadily, they gained on and then passed the other boats until only one remained in front of them – the boat carrying the Whiddy Crew.

Wielding their oars with quick, powerful strokes, the Caseys put the last measure of their stamina and the last iota of their incredible strength into the effort and with a final spurting lunge, drove their ancient boat forward to cross the finish line a mere boat length ahead of the exhausted Whiddy Crew.

While the Casey brothers hurried to beach their relic of a boat before it could fill with water and sink, they heard the local committee members calling out to the three other crews: 'What excuse now – you so-called champions from County Cork? You let these young fellows from County Kerry beat you in an old tub that we were afraid was going to sink.'

The Caseys tried their best to soften the blow to the Whiddy Crew's pride. After all, they told them, we're a lot younger than you are and that's got to count for something. The Whiddy Crew were gracious losers, proving themselves to be real sportsmen. After all, it was really not too shameful to come in second to this incredible crew of Casey brothers. One must remember they had beaten every other crew in Ireland that had gone against them. They simply did not know what it meant to lose.

Believe it or not, the seven Casey brothers were **never** beaten – by **anyone**.

SEVEN

BRANCHING OUT

Finding races in which to row was becoming more difficult for the Caseys. Racing committees eager for their own local champions to win, and knowing that crews would drop out of any competition the Caseys entered, began to 'gerrymander' their competitions. They would limit entries into their races to crews from towns within a specified radius of the site where the event was to be held. Somehow, the radius of that circle always seemed to exclude the town of Sneem. So the Casey brothers were unable to enter many races that they surely would have won.

This situation did not prevail for too long, however, for very quickly, the crowds which had followed the Caseys from race to race, began to dwindle and then disappear completely. Where once the spectators had numbered anywhere from 500 to 1,000, there were now only a handful of people in attendance. The Casey brothers were the big draw and without them the races were a financial bust. Regatta committees could not cover their expenses and the concession operators had food and drink going begging, for there were not enough people on hand to buy their wares and turn them a profit.

This situation was allowed to continue until it became intolerable. When it finally became clear that boat races without the Casey brothers were not going to attract any crowds at all, the race promoter at Waterville admitted defeat and made a concession to the Caseys. He approached Big Mick with a proposition: he would allow the Casey brothers to enter his races but only on the condition that they would compete against one another. Big Mick considered this for a while and, in the end, he agreed but only on the condition that the total monetary compensation to the boys would remain as before. Eager to have the paying crowds return, the promoter agreed quickly. So it was that the Casey brothers found themselves racing against one another. Singles, doubles, four-oars, sixes – they raced in them all.

By this time, Steve, Paddy and Jack were working as lumberjacks for the local sawmill. Jim had a job as a gardener at the age of twelve and shortly thereafter he landed a job as a deck hand on Lord Dunraven's yacht *The Boneen*. He rowed a small boat to and from his job on Lord Dunraven's estate on Garnish Island each working day. (It's curious to note that Lord Dunraven was also the sponsor of two America's Cup entries, *Valkyrie II* in 1893 and *Valkyrie III* in 1895.)

Mick, Tom and Dan were still working at home at their principal occupation of fishing. When he was either eight or nine years of age, Dan contracted rheumatic fever, a disease that nearly cost him his life and which required three full months of recuperation.

It was in this same time period that Big Mick Casey extended his enterprise. In response to a demand for sand and gravel to be used in agricultural applications, Big Mick had a large shallow-draft boat built that would permit him to navigate up the river to where beach sand and gravel were available in great abundance. Again, the boys were pressed into service to cut the oak trees and plane the planks used in the boat's construction. This boat was 45 feet in length and some 12 feet wide. Its keel was ballasted with some five tons of steel and lead – abandoned material taken from ruined homes previously owned by English landowners that were destroyed in the War of Independence and the subsequent Civil War.

The boat held some thirty-five tons of sand that could be sold at a good price. However, there were a couple of catches. Firstly, the boat had to be sailed to the beachhead just before low tide and then beached upon the shore and braced with tons of sand around the bulwarks to keep the loaded sand from crushing the keel. Then the sand was loaded aboard, shovelful by shovelful. Eventually, the tide turned to wash away the restraining sand and free the boat for its return trip. When they reached their destination, the boat had to be off-loaded in the same way – thirty tons shovelful by shovelful. However, hauling the sand was a snap compared to the gravel. The gravel was washed up and deposited much further from the shoreline beyond the wide strip of sand. It had to be shovelled into a wheelbarrow that was wheeled down to the water's edge. The gravel was then transferred to a small boat that was rowed out to the larger boat and the gravel transferred. It was killing, backbreaking work but imagine, if you can, how it helped to build and strengthen the already incredible physiques of these untiring young men.

A further small catch to this enterprise was the timing of the tides. Regulated by the waxing and waning of the moon, the time of the tides varied significantly. It was not at all uncommon for Big Mick to wake the boys at ten or eleven o'clock at night to have them set sail (or row, if there was no wind or if the wind was unfavourable), so as to use the tides to best advantage. Then, after a full night of this incredibly hard labour, the boys had to stumble off to their daytime jobs, groggy from lack of sleep.

And as if their jobs, their boat racing and hauling sand and gravel were not enough to sap their energies or their competitive spirits, the boys indulged in yet another favourite form of Irish athletic competition: 'tug-of-war'. These matches consist of two teams, pulling on opposite ends of a rope, trying to pull the other team across a line drawn at the beginning of the match beneath the middle of the length of rope. In countries such as the United States, tug-of-war matches are generally limited to good-natured, almost comical, events at firemen's picnics, or staged over muddy ground by college fraternity members in the madness of spring, always with seven men to a side. But tug-of-war in Ireland was a deeply serious event. It was, in fact, the featured event of the day in all track and field competitions, with ten men to each side.

So the seven Casey brothers fielded a 'tug-of-war' team. For their other three members, they enlisted Mick Sullivan, Jack 'Tade' Sullivan (a cousin of their mother's) and, as their anchorman, Tom Sheehan. Tom was a giant of a man at 6 foot 4 inches tall and weighing 240 pounds. 'Big Mick' Sheehan, Tom's equally large brother, served as their coach and manager. 'Big Mick' Sheehan had been the All-Irish Champion in the single pull. The alternative team members were Mick Leary and Denny Leary.

Tug-of-War Power *(l–r):* Steve (anchor), Tom, Mick, Dan, Paddy and Jack. Drawing by Patricia Casey, Paddy's daughter.

One day in 1932, Big Mick Sheehan took his team to a meet in Kenmare. There the Casey brothers and their teammates were pitted against other very strong teams who provided stern tests of their strength. Along with their huge anchor, Tom Sheehan, the teammates planted their feet, dug in their heels and pulled mightily. They won match after match until they had advanced to the final pairing of the day. The team they faced in that final match consisted of ten huge men from the town of Mallow, County Cork, some 50 or 60 miles from Sneem, so the men were strangers to the Caseys.

The referee said, 'Ready, set, go.' and the rope snapped taut as twenty strong men pulled powerfully. Groaning, grunting, straining and digging in their feet, the Caseys and their teammates began to gain superiority over the opposing team. Inch by inch, they pulled the rope and the ten straining

The Munster Heavyweight Tug-of-War Championship Team, *back row (l–r)*: Denny Leary, Mick Sullivan, Jim Casey, Tom Casey, Steve Casey and Tom Sheehan (anchorman); *front row (l–r)*: Jack Casey, Mick Sheehan (coach), Dan Casey, Paddy Casey, Mick Leary and friend Mick Howley.

men toward them until, finally, they snapped them over the line, lurching and tripping as their resistance gave way.

As they were congratulating each other and smiling at well-wishers who were clapping their backs and shaking their hands, the Caseys heard Big Mick Sheehan saying, 'Well, boys, now you're the best there is in all of Munster.'

'What do you mean, the best in Munster?' the boys asked.

'Well, don't you know that you have just won the Munster Tug-of-War Championship?'

The boys hadn't known. They stood looking at one another and grinning as the realisation set in.

'Surely, you know that this Mallow team you have just beaten has won the Munster Championship for the last four years in a row?'

There were sheepish, surprised looks of delight on the faces of the brothers and their teammates. They hadn't known. They thought that this was just another match like so many others they had won in the past.

So here they were, the Casey brothers, champions at everything they had put their hands and backs to. By now they were so sure of themselves and issued a challenge that spread far and wide across the land: they challenged any other family of seven brothers – if such could be found – to take them on in any sport of their choosing – be it rowing, tug-of-war, wrestling or boxing. That they truly were unique is borne out by the fact that the only response they got to this challenge was from a team from near Killarney made up of seven cousins. The Caseys met this team in a tug-of-war match and beat them soundly and quickly.

The seven Casey brothers were flexing their muscles and were beginning to come of age.

EIGHT

'SCUFFLING' PAYS OFF

Ireland has a history of people sorrowfully leaving in search of a better life. The population of Ireland in 1846 was 8.25 million; by 1921, thanks to the potato famine (1845–1852) and the onset of financial depression, the population was down to 4.3 million. Many of the Irish emigrated to America, as had Mick Casey and Bridget Sullivan, at least for a while. These Irish immigrants were to provide for America much of the muscle and strength that were needed just then to build the railroads, the bridges and the subways. The Irish immigrant injected into America a good part of the work ethic that is found there still today.

During the Great Depression of the 1930s, many immigrants left Ireland for England as well. Although England was caught up in the worldwide decline in industry and had thousands of unemployed, it still provided better prospects for young men seeking their fortune than did Ireland.

Steve was the first of the Caseys to leave, breaking up the fraternity of brothers for the first time. He migrated to London in 1934, where he thought his chance of finding work would be best. Can you imagine the changed world he found there – he and his brothers after him – from the green

Three young Caseys on their way to sports fame *(l–r)* Paddy, Tom and Jim.

slopes and blue lakes and the gentle flowing rivers of the Emerald Isle, to crowded, smoky, industrialised London? It must have been difficult for him to make such an adjustment but adjust he did, and he soon found work on a construction crew that paid him a fair wage.

He also found the Ace Rowing Club that competed on the River Thames in Hammersmith in the heart of London.

A few months after Steve went to London, Paddy, Mick and Tom followed. They were also successful in finding jobs and soon they too had joined Steve in the Ace Rowing Club and were leading the club to many victories.

After they had been in London for a few months, Paddy and Steve heard about openings for jobs as 'bouncers' at the Bedford Hotel. They couldn't believe it – they were going to be paid for 'scuffling'. The club owner took one look at these fine physical specimens and hired them on the spot. Their job was to keep order in the hotel's club, which sometimes meant having to eject unruly customers who tried to start trouble.

Late one night, the two brothers were engaged in throwing three roughnecks out into the street. Once outside the club, the troublemakers turned on Steve and Paddy and began throwing punches. The boys got a little hot under the collar; Paddy picked up one of the tough guys and slammed him into the bonnet of a taxi that was parked at the side of the road. Steve, being the older brother, had to do him one better, so he picked his roughneck up, held him suspended in mid-air for a moment and then threw him over the roof of the taxi and nearly to the other side of the street (remember that in those days, motor vehicles stood taller than a man's head.)

As luck would have it, there were two men on the footpath that night who saw this prodigious display of strength and immediately became interested in the two Casey brothers. They were Mick Howley and Harold Angus, former Olympic welterweight wrestlers who were now wrestling professionally.

They approached Steve and Paddy – cautiously. They asked them if they were interested in doing some wrestling – they thought the boys might be good at it.

'Wrestling?' said the boys. 'What's that?'

'Well, you know, where you go into a ring with another fellow and each tries to get the other down on his back and pin him down.'

'Oh, that. We don't call that wrestling. We call that scuffling.'

'Well, whatever you call it, we think you might do well at it. Why don't you stop off at Klein's Gym some time? It's just a few streets from here.'

Soon, not only Steve and Paddy but also Mick and Tom were working out in Klein's Gym. The owner, 'Old Man' Klein, was a former champion wrestler who was now some seventy years old. Like Mick Howley and Harold Angus, he took a liking to the boys (most everyone did) and showed them a few fundamental holds and grips. The boys were permitted to come to the gym at any time, as it was open around the clock training both wrestlers and boxers. The boys generally came late at night or very early in the morning when they got off work.

Perhaps because of their earlier experience with 'scuffling', their great strength or innate athletic ability – or a combination of these – the boys proved to be quick studies and have a great deal of natural ability. Soon they were ready to enter amateur wrestling matches and, again, the brothers won, and won consistently.

(opposite) Tom Casey, who was spotted by fight manager and promoter Pat Dailey as a prospective champion. After just nine days' training he won the British Amateur Heavyweight Boxing Championship in 1937. However, persistent hand and knuckle injuries prevented him from achieving world fame.

Tom, however, was not to pursue a career in wrestling. One day as he pawed at another wrestler in the practice ring, he was spotted by one Pat Dailey, a very prominent fight manager and promoter of the day. He watched Tom carefully for a while and then approached him with the suggestion that he should turn to boxing rather than wrestling. He had observed the way that Tom handled himself; the quickness, balance, deftness and great strength, and his experienced eye told him that Tom could use these skills to better advantage in the boxing ring. Tom amiably agreed that he was game to try and so laced on a pair of boxing gloves for the first time in his life.

Incredible as it may seem, nine days later, Tom won the Amateur Heavyweight Boxing Championship. To say that Pat Dailey had spotted a great natural talent is an understatement of the highest order. If this achievement sounds incredible, let the reader remember that this and all the other Casey brother accomplishments have been documented and are a matter of record.

By the way, it is of interest to note that the fateful meeting of Mick Howley with Steve and Paddy Casey was to result in a life-long relationship with the Casey clan. Some years later, Mick Howley married Margaret Casey who, like her sisters Josephine and Catherine (Kitty), had left Sneem to travel to London in search of jobs and new opportunities. I must tell you too that, before leaving Ireland, all three Casey sisters competed in rowing. They rowed in both the singles and doubles at the Kenmare Regatta and were quite successful. So the Casey and Sullivan genes were not limited to the sons but were passed on to Margaret, Josephine and Kitty as well.

NINE

WHAT MIGHT HAVE BEEN

Duracy were members of the British amateur wrestling
team. They travelled with the team all over Europe, both of
them winning their matches consistently. In 1936, they left
the amateur ranks and began to wrestle professionally. They
both had a need for the extra money it would bring and
thought little of it. This move was to prove their undoing
later that year, when they were part of the Ace Rowing Club
in London that was participating in the All-England Rowing
Championships. The winners of this competition would
represent England in the 1936 Olympics that were to be held
in Berlin, Germany. Tom and Mick Casey were also in
training with the club and the four brothers competed
together in the four-oar sweeps and the quads.

Meanwhile, back in Ireland, Jim, Dan and Jack Casey
were also in training. They were prepared to join their
brothers so as to have Caseys competing in every type of
rowing match from the single sculls on up to the eight-oar
sweeps. Their first cousin Joe Casey was training with them
as coxswain. They trained in a unique kind of boat, one that
could be configured in many different ways: single scull;
double scull (two men with two oars each); two-oar sweeps

Steve Casey (*right*) squares up with former American Heavyweight Champion Jack Sharkey in Boston in 1935.

(two men with one oar each); four-oar sweeps (four men with one oar each); quads (four men with two oars each); and eight-oar sweeps (eight men with one oar each).

The Ace Rowing Club, featuring the rowing skills of Steve, Paddy, Tom and Mick Casey, won the All-England Rowing Championships and were preparing to go off to Germany for the Olympics.

Some might say that the Caseys were naive not to know that wrestling professionally would disqualify them from participation in the all-amateur Olympic competition. Well, perhaps that can be said of them. Perhaps they were naive but you have to remember that these were simple lads not far removed by time or distance from their humble beginnings. You must also remember that Olympic sport was not nearly as well known or appreciated then as it is today. At any rate, they were not aware of any wrongdoing; it never entered their minds that the two sports of wrestling and rowing were related in any way or that competing professionally in one would have any effect upon competing as amateurs in another.

The great American track star Jim Thorpe was equally naive; he won the 1912 Olympic Decathlon in Stockholm, Sweden, but had to surrender his gold medal later when it was learned that he had been paid for playing baseball prior to his participation in the Olympics. In 1982, after Thorpe's death, the International Olympic Committee restored his medal.

Jack Kelly Sr was a great oarsman who entered the Diamond Sculls in England years before with an eye toward winning an Olympic berth. He was disqualified, not because he was a professional athlete but because he worked for a living – he was a bricklayer who later founded a construction empire but he was disqualified only because he earned money at another enterprise. Later, his son John made it to the Olympics, winning the Diamond Sculls in England to qualify.

Though the Casey brothers might have been ignorant of their 'professional' status in 1936, someone else was not and complained to the authorities that Steve, Paddy and Tom had been in professional wrestling and boxing matches. As a consequence, the Ace Rowing Club entry was disqualified and the team they had beaten in the All-England

Championships went to Berlin to represent the United Kingdom.

There has never been any doubt in the minds of any of the Caseys or of their many supporters what the outcome would have been had they been able to compete in the rowing events in Berlin in 1936. They were confident that they would have won all six of the rowing events – a feat unparalleled in the history of the Olympics. The Caseys would have set the boating world on its ear and would have shown the world what seven superbly conditioned Irish brothers could achieve. If the Caseys had competed, they would have taken home gold medals.

However, it was not to be, and the three Caseys who had stayed behind in Ireland were upset because they were not called upon to step in and fill the ranks when their older brothers were disqualified. After all, they said, there are always more Caseys at home.

TEN

ON THEIR WAY TO GLORY

After their terrible disappointment of 1936, the brothers began to go their separate ways. But three of them were to be reunited in the not too distant future to win yet another glorious rowing event – this one in the United States.

Let us consider now the path that each Casey brother began to take, each to pursue, in his own way, his individual dream.

Dan and Jack Casey remained in Ireland, their active competitive careers essentially over. Dan, the youngest of the boys, remained on the old farm with his mother and father. Jack soon married and became a farmer. There will be more said about the personal lives of Jack and Dan and, indeed, of all the Caseys, in a later chapter.

As to Dan: his brothers all agreed that he was probably the best and strongest oarsman of them all.

Meanwhile, Steve, Paddy and Tom had all become full-blown professional athletes – Steve and Paddy were wrestlers and Tom was a boxer.

Tom's boxing career was progressing nicely. He had a number of fights that he won handily. However, he was troubled with a problem with his hand that may have stemmed from improper taping by his corner-men when he

Tom Casey (*right*) shown with the boxer Jack Pettifer, whom he defeated at Killarney in 1937.

was just starting out. Or, maybe it was just a reflection of how hard he could hit. His brother, Jim, sparred with him a few times and recalls that he could not eat comfortably for two days thereafter. Whatever the cause, Tom was constantly breaking his knuckles and the small bones in the back of his hands. He would win a fight and then have to wait until his hands were healed well enough to go again. It may well be that, in his anxiety to get into the ring and fight again, he just did not wait long enough between bouts for his hands to heal properly. That was typical of the Caseys – they wanted to get into action as soon and as often as they could, so that they could win.

Tom had a knockout punch, to be sure. There is the tale often told of his match with the sparring partner of the great Tommy Farr. It ended abruptly when Tom knocked him out very early in the first round.

Meanwhile, Steve and Paddy Casey embarked upon paths that, as we shall see in the following chapters, would lead to greatness.

What of young Jim Casey? Well, young Jim had left Ireland and had made his way to London too. He had been thinking that he would stay on in Ireland with his good job on Lord Dunraven's yacht but fate would have it otherwise. Jim felt particularly secure in his job and with his future prospects after having fished Lady Dunraven out of the water after she had fallen between a boat and a pier. Although the water was relatively shallow, and she was never in any real danger, she ever after proclaimed to all who would listen that Jim Casey had heroically saved her life.

News of the exploits of his brothers in England reached Jim and he was excited but also anxious to get in on the fun and the fame. His brothers were rowing, boxing and wrestling – without him. He just had to go and get in on some of this.

So, taking a week's pay and telling no one but his mother, Jim slipped off to London. He didn't contact his brothers immediately as he wanted to get some wrestling experience under his belt first, so that he could meet them on something like his own terms. He wanted to prove to himself that he was capable in the wrestling ring. Later, when he was sparring with his brother Paddy, he realised that this hadn't helped him very much. Jim was wearing headgear to protect his ears, which had been damaged and which were already becoming 'cauliflowered'. Paddy gripped Jim in such a vicious headlock that the straps of his headgear were broken: the ear-cup over his right ear became dislodged and his ear was ripped off. It hung in shreds and sixteen stitches were needed to reattach the ear. Playful fellows, these Caseys.

So Jim got a job in London demolishing buildings. (Did the Casey boys ever have anything but backbreaking jobs?) He would work all day at breaking up reinforced concrete with a sledgehammer and then go over to Klein's Gym to work out at nine or ten o'clock at night – staying until one or two in the morning. He paid five shillings a week for the use of the gym and began to pick up some pointers from some of the experienced wrestlers and trainers who congregated there.

One night, after Jim had been working out for two or three weeks, a young man made an entrance that caused quite a stir in the gym. The stranger turned out to be Benny Engleblum, the Finnish light-heavyweight Olympic wrestling champion – a man with a fearsome reputation in the ring. He was looking for a workout.

One of the regulars agreed to take him on for a round or two. It didn't last a full found. The Finn slammed the fellow to the mat so heavily that he lay there moaning for several minutes, unable to get up.

Paddy Lyons, a good Irish amateur wrestler who had befriended Jim and who outweighed Benny Engleblum by a good 30 pounds, decided he would give it a try. In very short order, Benny put him out.

Knowing by now, as you do, the competitive nature of the Caseys, it will come as no surprise to learn that, at this point, Jim Casey said, 'Let me have a shot at him.'

'You?' said the trainer. 'You've been wrestling for all of two weeks and this fellow's an Olympic champion.'

'I don't care who he is. I want a shot at him.'

'Okay, it's your funeral. Go ahead and get your head snapped off.'

So Jim got into the ring with the Finnish champion. Engleblum tried to use the same tactic he had used on the first two men but Jim was ready for him. Jim countered with a leg snatch that sent them both crashing to the canvas. Quick as a flash, Jim wrapped his leg around his opponent's body and an arm around his neck in such a way that the Finn was completely immobilised. After struggling futilely for a minute or so, the Finn finally said, 'That's enough,' and gave up.

Benny Engleblum was shocked. He took the trainer of to one side and said, 'My God, that man is strong. Who is he? How long has he been wrestling?'

'His name is Jim Casey, one of the Casey brothers, and I hate to tell you this, Benny, but he's only been wrestling for a few days.'

They had a few more words together and then the trainer came over to Jim. 'Casey, you're a natural born wrestler. Why don't I sign you to a five-year exclusive contract? I'll get you matches all over England, all over the world – America, Europe, Africa, and you'll make lots of money – thousands of pounds.'

That sounded pretty exciting to Jim, who was ready to sign on the spot, but Paddy Lyons stopped him. 'Jim, you'd better talk to your brothers before you take a step like that.' So, off went Paddy Lyons to tell Jim's brothers what Jim was thinking of doing.

Paddy Casey found Jim as quickly as he could and just as quickly talked Jim out of signing the contract. 'Don't you

sign anything with anybody. These fellas'll take everything and leave you nothing but sweat.' None of Jim's brothers – not Steve, nor Paddy, nor Tom – had ever signed a contract. They were suspicious of big-city promoters and, besides, where they came from, a man's word and a simple handshake were all that were ever needed.

So Jim began to take what bouts he could find, much as Steve and Paddy were doing.

Jim's first professional bout was in an exhibition match in Ireland. The benefit was to raise funds for the maintenance of the estate of the great Irish patriot Daniel O'Connell, in Derrynane, County Kerry. (Years later, when the American President John F. Kennedy toured Ireland and captured the hearts of the Irish people, the Irish government offered to make him a gift of the O'Connell estate and two other large estates as well. His tragic assassination the next year put an end to speculation that the young Irish-American might one day choose to become a landed Irish gentry man.)

Jim's match was with a very good heavyweight named Dave Armstrong. There was no winner or loser in this match; they were simply putting on an exhibition of wrestling.

After a couple of months, Jim found it necessary to quit his job. He was wrestling once or twice a week (until other promoters started to avoid him) and was travelling some distance to his matches – all over England and to Wales and Scotland as well.

(*opposite*) Paddy Casey was a tremendous athlete. Together with Steve, Tom and Mick he helped to win the All-England rowing championship in 1936 for the Ace Rowing Club and looked destined to compete in the Olympics in Berlin that year. But they were disqualified because Steve and Paddy had wrestled professionally. Until the day he died in February 2002, Paddy was adamant that they would have won numerous gold medals in those Olympic Games. He was the last of the seven brothers to die.

Like his brothers, Jim won consistently. Soon, the Casey brothers were having trouble getting matches. No one wanted to wrestle them – they were just too good. It was similar in many ways to their situation back in Ireland when they were 'gerrymandered' out of the boat races so that someone else would have a chance of winning.

So, did the Casey brothers take this treatment lying down? Surely you know the Caseys better than that by now.

ELEVEN

TRIUMPH

I could undertake to tell you how the Casey brothers resolved the problem of getting matches but the story was told in considerable detail by an eyewitness, a man who was personally involved in the story.

Gerald Egan was a fight promoter as well as a sports journalist in London in the 1930s. As you will see by reading an article he wrote, which I quote below, he was instrumental in launching the Caseys (and Steve in particular) on their fantastic wrestling careers.

The article appeared in the *Empire News* in London on 6 March 1955 and is a personal retrospective by Gerald Egan. The column is headlined: 'FIGHTING CASEYS SCARED 'EM ALL'.

The world famous quartet of wrestling Caseys from Sneem, County Kerry, are wealthy men today as a result of their success as wrestlers, but their achievements inside the ring might have been overshadowed by their triumphs outside the ropes if their story had been told before. For if anybody fought hard to get into the mat game, it was the Caseys. From the beginning of their careers – right after I discovered Steve working as a commissionaire at the door

Do You Want To Be A World Champion? Five of the brothers appear on
this promotional poster from the 1930s.

of a London Hotel in the autumn of 1934 – the Caseys were a crew so tough that no British wrestler wanted anything to do with them. Even when they were a bunch of novices, they proved themselves no respecters of names. One by one, they knocked off London's crowd-pulling glamour boys of the ring until they ran out of opponents.

This did not popularise them with the promoters, who had spent time and money building up their attractions. The result was that after less than a year in the game, the Caseys found themselves on the boycott list of most of the wrestling impresarios, who took the view that the Kerry men would soon return to Ireland.

Although there was big money for those in the game, the four Caseys, Steve, Paddy, Jim and Tom, had lean times but they were no quitters. They decided to force the promoters to give them their rights and although their methods were a little unorthodox, I must admit they were effective.

They launched their first attack on the hierarchy of British wrestling in January 1935 when Legs Longiven was billed to meet Shorty Scott for the British and Empire Heavyweight titles. For weeks London wrestling fans had been looking forward to the 'match of the year', for which there was a side stake of £250.

On the night of the event, the Vale Hall, in Northwest London was packed to capacity. The ring was more crowded than usual as celebrities jostled with managers, seconds and stakeholders every time the MC identified one of them for the pleasure of the crowd.

Then, just as the last celebrity was being introduced, Jim and Paddy Casey jumped into the ring. It was just as if

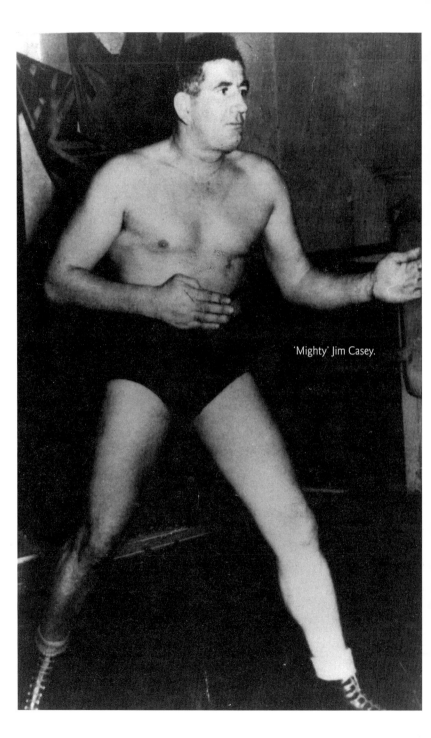

'Mighty' Jim Casey.

an earthquake had hit the building as the two six-footers lashed out at everybody who tried to stop them.

Pandemonium reigned as the boiled shirts scampered from the ring – many of them falling out headfirst. Even the seconds and the managers found a quick way out. The MC bolted so fast that he was all the way out the back exit before the others had had time to fall out of the ring.

The crowd went wild with delight. This was better than the pictures. And it was real life, too.

In about fifteen seconds the Caseys had cleared the ring except for the two title contenders who were looking very uncomfortable sitting on their corner stools.

Paddy Casey picked up the microphone and the audience listened quietly as Paddy told them that he and his brothers had been boycotted.

'The promoters and wrestlers have made the game a closed shop,' he said. Then Big Jim took the microphone and shouted his challenge so loud he could almost be heard in his native Kerry. 'We'll wrestle any ten men on this bill tonight,' he bellowed as he threw down the mike.

Then, like lightning, the two Kerry men whipped off their clothes and displayed their wrestling togs. Throwing the clothes to the timekeeper, they made for the two title contenders.

With that, the wrestlers were not sitting on their stools any more. They were running just as fast as the boiled shirt brigade had done a few minutes earlier.

That was only one of the many onslaughts the Caseys made on the sport of wrestling until the promoters decided it was easier to work with them than against them.

Paddy and his three brothers got all the wrestling matches they required but against leading continental

Steve 'Crusher' Casey.

wrestlers who were too good for the British stars. It was by licking the best European mat men that the Caseys first earned their fame in England. Shortly afterwards, I started promoting in Ireland. I featured them in my shows. At once, Steve proved to be a sensation. He introduced his Killarney Flip, which rendered his opponents helpless. At the end, I was finding it hard to get him opponents, with the result that I advised him to go to America. 'I am going to the States shortly,' I told him, 'and I'll speak to Paul Bowser, the Boston promoter, for you.'

(In reminiscing about the Caseys): Steve trained hard and soon found it difficult to find sparring partners. The only ones who could give him a real workout at the end of the three months' training were Paddy, Jim and Tom, his three tough brothers.

They, too, improved with practice and before the year was out they had scared the lives out of Britain's best wrestlers. The press soon caught on to the fighting sons of Kerry and when it became known that there were three other brothers – Mick, Dan and Jack – still in Ireland, they were saluted as being 'the toughest family on earth'. They became the most publicised sporting family in Ireland.

As wrestlers they reached the summit. Jim and Tom went to America with Steve in 1938 and made fortunes with their mitts ... Tom also did very well as a boxer.

Gerald Egan is unable to suppress the feeling of awe he had for the Casey brothers in this article written thirty-five years ago and concerning events that had happened in 1934, twenty-one years before that date.

He repeated the title which, even in the mid-1930s, was already being applied to this fantastic set of brothers and which we can see now they so richly deserve – 'the toughest family on earth'.

TWELVE

'CRUSHER CASEY'

True to his word, Gerald Egan contacted the fight promoter Paul Bowser in Boston. Jack McGraw, who acted as a 'talent scout' for Bowser, had also recommended that Bowser take Casey into his stable of wrestlers. So, in 1936, Steve Casey was off to America, to Boston where his father Big Mick Casey had rowed and brawled so many years before. He lived in Dorchester with an aunt and uncle and immediately began training for matches in Boston and New York.

He was an immediate sensation; a likeable Irishman in a town full of Irishmen. He won match after match against many of the established wrestlers of the day – men such as Rube Wright and Charlie Strack. His 'Killarney Flip', which he had invented and perfected, is difficult to describe and really had to be seen to be appreciated. Suffice it to say, that his opponents would find themselves caught in what they thought to be a conventional hold and would begin to think about conventional ways of breaking it, when they would suddenly find themselves airborne, sailing at high velocity across the ring, then crashing to the canvas on their backs. Before they could stop bouncing, Steve would crash his full weight upon them, pinning them to the canvas in crushing leg and arms grips as firm as steel vices.

World Champion Wrestler Steve Casey
Arrives in Boston

'Irish' Steve Casey is welcomed to Boston in 1936 by aunts, uncles, cousins and friends. The promoter Paul Bowser stands next to Steve with his hat in his hand.

The sporting press was given to dreaming up descriptive names for wrestlers and boxers no less in those days than in the present and soon the Boston papers were filled with glowing accounts of the wrestling skill and brute strength of the man they called Steve 'Crusher' Casey.

Later on, the American media referred to Jim Casey as either 'Thunderbolt' or 'Mighty' Casey and to Paddy as the 'Tiger of the Mat'. None of the names were concocted by the

Caseys or the members of their camp; the media bestowed them gratuitously and the athlete was stuck with them.

By 1938, Steve 'Crusher' Casey had fought in dozens of matches and had won them all. His record was such that he could no longer be ignored by the loose hegemony of promoters and managers who, in those days, decided who would meet whom in championship matches or who would be declared the new champion if a champion were to vacate his title.

Thus it was the case that on Saturday 11 February 1938, Steve 'Crusher' Casey met the reigning heavyweight champion of the world in a packed Boston Garden. The champion was Lou Thesz, a magnificent physical specimen and a true credit to the sport of wrestling. He always fought cleanly, bravely and well, and had an enviable record of ring triumphs stretching over many years. He was a seasoned veteran going against a twenty-nine-year-old who had only been wrestling for some four years.

In those days, it was the vogue to have a sports celebrity act as referee for the championship matches and for this match, the promoters had secured the services of the greatest American sports hero of the day – the great George Herman 'Babe' Ruth. A former star pitcher for the Boston Red Sox baseball team, 'Babe' had become a legendary player for the New York Yankees. Dubbed the 'Sultan of Swat' by the New York tabloids, Ruth's home run record of sixty, which he set in 1927, would stand until 1961, when Roger Maris, another Yankee, would eclipse it with sixty-one.

Ruth's presence in the ring was meant to generate more interest and sell more tickets to Steve Casey's fight but he was not really needed. Boston had taken the young Irishman

Ronnie Delany travelled to Sneem in 2002 to unveil a statue of Steve 'Crusher' Casey. In 1938 Steve was crowned Heavyweight Wrestling Champion of the World and retained the title for nine years until he retired, undefeated, in 1947. He is the only Irishman ever to retain a world title in any discipline for such an extended period of time. (Courtesy MacMonagle Photographers)

to heart and its citizens came out in droves to cheer him on in his pursuit of the world champion's belt.

The match, like all others of the day, was decided by the best two out of three falls or pins. There were no rounds, per se, just a short resting period granted after each fall, and there was no time limit. Some bouts had been known to go on for four or five hours before one man could manage his second and deciding fall.

One of the very last photographs of Paddy Casey, taken at the unveiling of the statue of Steve in Sneem by Ronnie Delany in 2002. (Courtesy MacMonagle Photographers)

Such was not the case in the Boston Garden that cold night in 1938.

At the bell, the two wrestlers circled each other cautiously for several minutes, feeling each other out. They tentatively tried a succession of holds, seeing how the other would react and the defence he would use. They tried tripping and butting and leg and arm grips designed to send a man off-balance and vulnerable to a movement that would send him crashing to the canvas. For thirty-five minutes they struggled, strength against strength, cunning against guile. Then suddenly Steve saw an opening, caught Thesz relaxing and overpowered him. Pinning his shoulders to the mat, he

Lou Thesz, whom Steve Casey defeated for the World Heavyweight title
in the Boston Garden on 11 February 1938.

looked up at Babe Ruth who was down on his knees looking on intently. 'One, two, three,' the Babe's ham-sized hands slapped the canvas. The first fall had gone to the Irish challenger.

After a short rest, the bout resumed. This time, the champion was a little more cautious. He now knew that Steve Casey was the strongest and quickest man he had ever faced. One more fall and the jewel-encrusted belt he had fought so hard to win would be gone, snatched away by this powerful young Irishman.

This time, the champion avoided the steel grasp of Steve 'Crusher' Casey for forty minutes. However, by the end of that time, he was beginning to tire and stagger. Seizing that opportunity, Steve smashed him to the mat, pinned him and again heard the great Babe Ruth slap out 'One, two, three.'

Steve 'Crusher' Casey was the new Heavyweight Wrestling Champion of the World.

From a family of champion stock bred in the rocks and mists of County Kerry had emerged a world champion. From the loins of 'Big' Mick Casey and the loving heart of Bridget Sullivan had come a brawling, scuffling, fighting, wrestling champion – a man who was acknowledged the world over as the world's finest wrestler. How far had he come, using only his God-given talent and strength and the fantastic competitive urge that was shared by all the Caseys and whose life-long war cry was always, 'Win, win, win.'

Though he was accustomed to winning and being a champion, Steve took nothing for granted. Whether in racing sculls, capturing the Salter Cup, winning the Munster Tug-of-War or on the hard canvas floor of boxing and wrestling arenas, he and his brothers were all great champions

Steve 'Crusher' Casey pinning Ernie Dusek in the late 1930s. Ernie Dusek
was born in Omaha, Nebraska, in 1909 and died in 1994.

and had won cups and crowns before. However, Steve Casey
had now won a world title and in a family of champions, he
had become the premier champion.

The laurels rested easily and naturally on his handsome
head.

THIRTEEN

BROTHERS IN BOSTON

Meanwhile, back in London, Paddy, Jim and Tom Casey were earning laurels of their own, although injuries would soon force Paddy and Tom to cut short their careers.

I have already recounted Tom's recurring difficulty with broken bones in his hands. When his hands were healed, he was a holy terror in the ring, as his father might have said. However, after each fight he was forced to endure a long period of healing before he could compete again. The doctors told him that the only way they could effect a permanent solution would be to encase his hands in a plaster cast all the way up to his forearms, completely immobilising the bones for several months, but this would mean that Tom could not work, could not make a living and so he had to forego this suggested treatment. Needless to say, he kept on boxing and winning.

In time, he had fought his way to the top of the European competition. In very short order, he became both the British and European heavyweight boxing champion. If his hands had not been so badly damaged, it is not inconceivable to think that he might have had a shot at the World Heavyweight title but as time and tide wait for no man, the highly competitive world of boxing could not wait for Tom Casey to heal, nor take a chance on having a champion who could defend his crown perhaps only once or twice a year, so that possibility passed him by. However, he had done superbly well in his chosen sport and, like his brother Steve, he wore his laurels gracefully and proudly.

Jim and Paddy Casey, after having shaken up the English wrestling world with their defiant challenge in the ring at Vale Hall on that memorable night, continued to wrestle whomever they could get to oppose them and continually won those matches. With no new worlds to conquer, since English promoters were still begrudging them matches and with their brother Steve now the World Champion, their attention turned to America and the opportunities that might lie there.

Accordingly, plans were made for all three brothers, Paddy, Jim and Tom, to return to America with their brother Steve, who had returned to Ireland on a visit in that same year of 1938. Fate intervened, however, to keep one of them from sailing.

One night, Paddy and Jim were featured on the same wrestling card at an arena in Manchester. Both won their matches but on the ride home, Paddy complained of a terrible pain in his back. When doctors examined him, they found that his back was broken and that his spinal cord was severely damaged. Here is yet again another demonstration of the toughness of the Caseys. Paddy's back had been broken sometime during the course of his match, yet he went on to win the match, showered and dressed and was on his way home before he admitted to feeling any pain. Tough? The word falls far short of describing the fortitude that Paddy Casey shared with his brothers.

On board the *President Harding: (l–r):* Steve, the captain and Tom Casey.

Both Steve and Jim had their backs broken in the course of their wrestling careers. They were fortunate, however, in that their spinal columns were not affected. Both returned to wrestling after a term of hospitalisation and a period of time for healing. All three of them suffered numerous bone breaks during their careers but Paddy's injury was the only one serious enough to end a career.

So Paddy's plans had to be changed and only Tom and Jim would accompany Steve on the return trip to the United States.

The three of them sailed from Cobh, County Cork, for America on the liner *President Harding*. During their Atlantic crossing, the three Caseys won the hearts of the crew and of their fellow passengers who were awed to have the world's champion wrestler and his brothers on board. The three Caseys obliged their newfound friends by putting on wrestling and boxing exhibitions. The ballroom was packed from wall to wall for each of the shows.

Landing in New York, the brothers were obliged to cool their heels at the immigration offices on Ellis Island, as had so many thousands of their countrymen before them. Before they were granted visas to stay in the United States, their uncles were required to post a security bond, pledging that these young Irishmen were not going to become wards of society or a burden on the community. The visas had to be renewed every six months for two years, at which time new visas had to be arranged. The boys adopted a pattern of arranging a match in Canada at the end of their two-year visa periods, remaining in Canada for a day or two and then re-entering the United States on the Canadian immigration quota.

FOURTEEN

NEW WORLDS TO CONQUER

Once away from Ellis Island, Steve, Tom and Jim were off to Dorchester to the home of their aunt and uncle. Now there were three Caseys running loose in Boston.

They all set out to get as many matches as possible and they continued their winning ways and were all known as crowd pleasers. Wherever they fought, the house was packed. Among others in this period, they fought the Dusek brothers from New York; three brothers against three brothers. Steve wrestled Ernie Dusek and won; Jim wrestled Rudy Dusek and won; Tom wrestled Emil Dusek but was disqualified for – what else? – punching. Tom just couldn't throw off his old boxing habits when he got excited.

On another occasion, the three Casey brothers were pitted against three brothers from Italy – 'the Great Garibaldis'. At the end of the evening, they had lost some of their 'greatness'. All three lost to the Casey boys. Steve beat Gino, Jim beat Ralph and the name of the third brother, who went down to defeat at the hands of Tom Casey, is lost in history. You can bet that that particular Garibaldi remembers Tom's name.

Tom also boxed from time to time, as the condition of his hands permitted. On one occasion, he fought a ranked heavyweight in the Boston Garden. With Tom's first punch, he broke his hand again but he was game enough to continue fighting despite the pain and also to avoid losing the fight. It was judged as a draw.

Tom's last fight took place in New Hampshire in 1939. A unique card was put together featuring Steve defending his title against Gud Sonnenberg, Jim in another wrestling match and Tom in a boxing match. They all trained in a rustic camp in the New Hampshire woods for three or four weeks prior to the matches. People came by the hundreds to watch them train. On the night of the match, all three brothers won handily. Tom won his fight by a knockout – a fitting finish to a brilliant boxing career. After this, Tom never boxed again, but he did wrestle occasionally.

Steve Casey had to vacate his world title on two occasions. The first time he was forced to do so was after his back was broken and major surgery was needed to repair a ruptured disc. Sandor Szabo was declared the champion in Steve's absence.

The second occasion was brought on by the same back injury. In the Second World War, Steve enlisted in the United States Army, in the Seacoast Artillery Branch. One day while on a mine laying exercise at sea, one of his shipmates became entangled in a steel cable and was dragged overboard with the huge cylindrical mines. Without hesitation, Steve went into the water to help him. In fighting to release the man from the cable, Steve was rammed in the back by one of the steel spikes that protruded from the mine's round surface and that also acted as a detonator when struck by a ship's hull. Fortunately, the mine did not explode but the damage to Steve's previously injured back was so severe that he had to

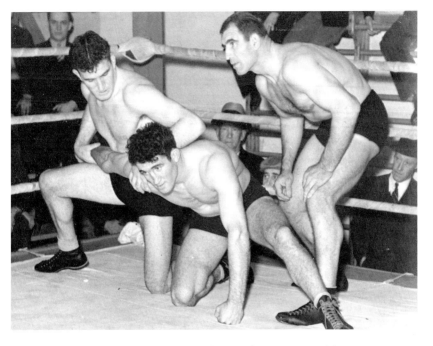

Three Casey brothers in action in the ring, *(l–r)*: Jim, Tom and Steve.

undergo surgery and vacate the title. This time the wrestling powers that be settled on Frank Sexton as the man to wear the vacated crown. Oddly enough, the man who could have, and many say most certainly should have, been awarded the title in this instance, was none other than Steve's younger brother, Jim Casey. We will go into these circumstances in more depth a little later in the story.

A Second World War vintage photo *(l–r):* Ed Don George (who represented America in freestyle wrestling in the 1928 Olympics in Amsterdam), Boston-based wrestling promoter Paul Bowser and Steve Casey.

FIFTEEN

THE GOVERNOR'S CUP

When Steve arrived in America, he joined the Riverside Boat Club in Cambridge, Massachusetts, and won many races there. It was just as natural as breathing that Jim and Tom, on arriving in Boston, became members too. The Riverside Boat Club members were all experienced oarsmen; many of them had been Olympic champions but none of them had ever seen the like of the Caseys.

Soon the Caseys' reputation became so formidable that they were having trouble getting competition – that complaint should sound familiar at this stage. So, at the suggestion of a journalist named Victor Jones, these confident young Irishmen posted a notice in *The Boston Globe* challenging any four men in the country, or in the world, to a race in either the four-oar sweeps or the quads. It was their intent, should the challenge be accepted, to have either Dan, Mick or Jack come over to America as their fourth crew member.

The boys said in their challenge that they would race anyone, whether amateur or professional – for any amount of money that they may be willing to put up. As the Caseys put it, they would race for 'money, marbles or chalk'. They just wanted to race.

The triumphant Caseys in their single sculls *(l–r):* Tom, Jim and Steve on the Charles River, Boston, Massachusetts.

Word of the challenge spread like wildfire across the country and around the world. Within the six-week limit they had established, four teams responded. One, sponsored by the City of Philadelphia, was Kelly's Boat Club. This Kelly was the fabulously wealthy Philadelphian who, years before, had been barred from Olympic competition because he was a bricklayer. He was also the father of the future screen star Grace Kelly (she would later become Princess Grace of Monaco). Kelly's son, also named John, had rowed in the 1936 Olympics four years before, as I have already recounted.

Another team that accepted the challenge was from Poughkeepsie in New York, another was from Canada. The fourth was from either Mexico or a South American country. As it turned out, their exact identities didn't matter.

Before the race, the Casey brothers made a tactical error that they should not have made if they were really serious about this race. They practiced their rowing on the Charles River in broad daylight – in full view of onlookers standing along the banks. Many of those who watched were from the challenging teams. They all had stopwatches and would click them as the Caseys began their run and snap down the stems as they crossed the finish line. Then they would glance at the time, shake their watches to be sure they were running properly and then shake their heads in disbelief. The times they were making were incredible. By now, a tremendous amount of interest had been generated all over the east coast by this upcoming challenge race and these four teams stood to lose more than just the side-stake if they were to lose to the Caseys. What their stopwatches told them was that they were surely going to lose. So, one by one they dropped out, withdrawing their acceptance of the challenge.

American rowing champion Russell Codman of The Union Boat Club, Boston, and Jim Casey following a training session at Jim's home on a man-made lake in Dickinson, Texas.

So, here was all of New England and the Atlantic seaboard primed for an exciting race and all the would-be competitors had backed down. Was there no one man enough to accept their challenge? There was such a man. A lone man – not a team. His name was Russell Codman, a sportsman who can be placed in the same league with the Caseys. He had just recently been placed second in the National Singles Championships.

Codman declared, 'It's a shame that these men, who would rather race than eat, can't get anyone to race them.' He said that he was willing to take them on but in singles rather than in quads and he was willing to post a considerable side bet. The Caseys, grateful for his sportsmanlike intervention, said that he need not chance so much money on the outcome and that 'marbles or chalk' would be fine. Codman, however, insisted that the bet should stand.

At this point, the Governor of Massachusetts, himself a fine sportsman, became involved. He announced that he would present an appropriately engraved silver loving cup to the winner of the race. He was Leverett Saltonstall, a member of a great Massachusetts family – a truly distinguished governor who went on to serve the people of his state as a highly respected member of the United States Senate. After his generous offer of this very expensive cup, the challenge became known as the Governor's Cup race.

On the appointed day for the race, 10 November 1940, it was estimated that 250,000 people lined the banks of the Charles River. The Caseys in their single sculls were off the mark like a shot at the crack of the starter's gun. After ten or fifteen strokes, Codman had already been left a length behind. Tom took the early lead, with Jim chasing him and trying to hold him back, not wanting to embarrass the

The Casey-Codman Challenge 1940
1st-Tom, 2nd-Jim, 3rd-Steve & 4th-Russell Codman

Steve, Tom and Jim admire the Governor's Cup, which they had just won in November 1940.

challenger who was madly rowing in an effort to catch up. There was no holding Tom back. His clean, swift strokes were eating up the river. At this point, all thoughts of the challenger faded. It became a race between the Casey brothers alone. Recognising this, Jim put his arms and his back into it and managed to cross the finish line half a length behind Tom, with the reigning World Heavyweight Wrestling Champion Steve Casey finishing closely behind. Russell Codman, game though he was, recognised early on in the race that he had no chance at all and simply rested on his oars and stared in open-mouthed amazement at the speed and form of the three Caseys.

The crowd erupted in an earth-shaking, shattering roar as the Caseys crossed the finish line. They could not believe what they had seen. Governor Saltonstall, in presenting the cup, was enthusiastic in his praise of their skill and strength. Crowds of well-wishers, including Ambassador Joseph Kennedy and his large family (all of whom were avid sportsmen who particularly loved water sports) were there to shake their hands and to slap their backs as they accepted the cup from Governor Saltonstall. Jim Casey particularly remembers John Kennedy, a seemingly shy young Harvard man who grinned a great deal. Russell Codman, grinning and still shaking his head in amazement, was there to congratulate them too.

Today that cup – still glistening and engraved with the names of the triumphant Caseys and the name of the Governor who presented it – rests in a trophy case in Jim Casey's home in Texas.

The members of the Riverside Boat Club loved to row with the Caseys and had always wondered just how good they really might be. As has been mentioned earlier, these were all men who excelled at rowing and several of them were past Olympic champions. These included the Whatner twins, Billy and Harry, and Jerry Shea. At that time, these were men of some fifty-five or sixty years of age. They had suspected for some time that the Caseys only rowed as hard as they needed to in order to win. This was undoubtedly so. Mick Casey had conditioned them years before to win by only as much as was needed.

These older men were awed by the power, grace and speed of the Casey brothers. Jerry Shea rowed with the three of them once and came back to report the experience to the others: 'I tell you, I didn't add a thing to that crew. It's as if I wasn't even there. I managed to keep stroke with them but just as my oars would start to bite the water, the boat would surge ahead from the might of their strokes and my oars were just following through – not adding any power at all. I tell you, they're unbelievable.'

The members were insistent on knowing just how fast the brothers really were and so it was that the three Casey brothers lined up at the start of a 2,000-metre course in single sculls. This time there was only a clock to beat but that particular clock had not been beaten for thirty-eight years. A man named Greer, who had died a few years before, had set the course record of six minutes and fifty-seven seconds in 1902 and his record still stood in 1940.

Not for long. Now the Caseys could row flat out with no holding back and indeed they did. They rowed like demons yet with the same silken stroke and upright posture that had always characterised their style. Wetted oars flashing in the wintry sunlight, whirlpools swirling in their shimmering wakes, they moved like water bugs skating on a mirrored surface.

'The Toughest Family on Earth', *back row (l–r):* Jim, Steve, Mick and Tom; *front row (l–r):* Jack, Paddy and Dan.

They burst past the finish line, Jim in the lead by half a length, then Tom, then Steve. The Riverside Boat Club members looked at their stopwatches, looked again and then looked at one another in astonishment.

Jerry Shea turned to Billy Whatner: 'Billy, what do you think of that?'

Billy answered, 'Shea, it was never done in that time before and it will never be done again.'

The awed Riverside Boat Club members, those grizzled veterans of Olympics past, compared the times on their stopwatches with one another and whistled and stomped with glee. The Caseys had beaten the course record – a record that had stood for thirty-eight years – by a full twenty-two seconds. Their time: six minutes, thirty-five seconds. Billy Whatner was right – it had never been done before and would never be done again.

SIXTEEN

'MIGHTY' JIM CASEY

I have said a number of times in this account that there was very little difference to be noted between the seven Casey brothers when it came to strength or toughness or ability. One brother might have beaten another in any given sport on any given day, only to turn around the next day and be beaten himself by that selfsame brother. Far be it from me to declare that one was superior to another in any respect.

I am compelled to say, however, that Jim Casey tried his hand at, and succeeded at, a few more enterprises than did his brothers. One might say, he was a little more venturesome. His life story is studded with experiences that make him stand out somewhat among the brothers. After all, he was the one who trained and coached NASA's shuttle astronauts in the tug-of-war. He led them to victory after victory. It is because of that diversity of interest that Jim's story fills so many of these pages. He protested to me that too much space is devoted to him but I will leave it to the reader to decide which of these interesting stories concerning Jim Casey, would **you** have left out?

Let us go back to where we last left Jim – in 1940 he won the Governor's Cup and then he set the course rowing record.

By late 1940, Jim was becoming a pretty big drawing card at the wrestling arenas but he found himself resting naturally enough in the shadow of his oldest brother Steve. Steve was, after all, the Heavyweight Wrestling Champion of the World. As they lived together, it was convenient for them to be booked together, however, Jim was never going to get anything other than second billing and smaller purses while wrestling on the same card as Steve. So Jim made a few telephone calls to promoters on the west coast of America. He found that these gentlemen were delighted to hear he was coming west and promised he would have no trouble getting bookings there.

So, in late 1940 or early 1941, Jim left Boston and headed for California. A friend of his, Danno O'Mahoney, a former world champion wrestler from County Cork, was living with his wife and four children in Santa Monica, California. Jim went to stay with them and lived with them, off and on, for several years. Later, when Jim settled and Danno was moving about the country, Jim was able to reciprocate by providing him with lodgings. Danno, known as the 'Irish Whip' in the wrestling arena, had beaten Jimmy Londos (the 'Golden Greek') for the heavyweight crown in 1935. Still a fearsome wrestler, he was nonetheless a kind and gentle man who helped Jim Casey considerably in his early days on the west coast.

The O'Mahoney home was located on Santa Monica Boulevard, across the street from The Irish Whip, Danno's bar, and just a short distance from the Santa Monica beach, the famed 'Muscle Beach' that was generally populated by weightlifters, bodybuilders, boxers and wrestlers and a sprinkling of film stars who were interested in keeping fit. This was an ideal place for Jim to get into shape for resuming his wrestling career: he was slightly run down and under-weight after his training for the Governor's Cup race. He spent four or five hours a day on the beach, running and swimming. He generally ran 6 or 7 miles a day; sometimes he ran as far as 30 miles – 15 miles down the beach and back again. In those days, the beach frontage was open – such a run could not be made today.

Many of the men who frequented the beach were willing to give Jim a sparring match as he worked to sharpen his wrestling skills. His name was well known and many of these amateur athletes were thrilled to have the opportunity to associate with this famous man – several of the leading men of Hollywood were among them. Among others, Jim sparred with and gave instructions to Gary Cooper, Clark Gable and Burt Lancaster. (These were much different times than we know today. Can you imagine the chaos that would ensue today if three such famous movie celebrities were to appear on a public beach?) Gable and Lancaster had both wrestled in the amateur ranks before going on to find fame and fortune on the silver screen. Burt Lancaster, in particular, was strong and very quick but he had an advantage as he was once a circus acrobat. As for Gary Cooper – with his skinny frame, it was mostly a case of wishful thinking. Danno O'Mahoney frequented the beach too but he didn't work out. An inveterate reader, he would lie on a lounge chair for hours reading a book. To his big toe he had attached a string and tied its other end to the leg of his youngest son, 'Punchy'. The string was just long enough to permit the boy to reach the water's edge and no further.

There were a lot of young boys who played on this beach too and wherever Jim Casey went in those days he was surrounded by kids. Everywhere he went, he went out of his

Jim Casey giving final instruction to Roger Sampson *(left)* and Bobby Lundeen *(right)* before one of their exhibition matches. Note that the MC seems to be protecting the microphone.

way to befriend young boys and teach them the rudiments of wrestling, boxing and physical fitness. All his life he was to have a knack for spotting athletic potential and developing it. On 'Muscle Beach', as elsewhere, he found a group of young lads who were delighted to receive his attention and instruction.

Among the crowd of boys on the beach he found two youngsters, both just eight years old, who were particularly gifted athletically and who learned quickly. When he resumed wrestling, he took these two boys, Roger Sampson and Bobby Lundeen, along with him. During the intermission at the matches, Jim would introduce them and announce that they would give an exhibition of wrestling, with Jim refereeing. The crowd thoroughly enjoyed the efforts of these two fine young lads and showed their appreciation (after some urging from Jim) by throwing money into the ring for them. After a while, the boys had amassed a considerable amount of money and other wrestlers, thinking that Jim must be lining his own pockets, began to imitate him – some with their own sons. What they didn't know, or wouldn't believe, was that Jim had opened bank accounts for Roger and Bobby in their own names and had never kept a cent of the money for himself.

Jim even issued challenges at these intermission exhibitions for any young lads in the house, up to the age of twelve, to try his luck against one of the boys. Several did but though some were older, they could not escape from the holds that Jim had taught his star pupils. Once, while at 'Muscle Beach', a wrestler named Abe Cashey brought his son along. The boy was about twelve, weighed in at about 140 pounds and, it can be assumed, had had a few professional pointers from his father. Cashey proposed that his boy wrestle one of Jim's pupils – perhaps wanting to show Jim up for some reason. Nine-year-old Roger, who weighed no more than 70 pounds, took on the challenger. For a few minutes they grappled in the sand, then Roger applied a quick arm-lock on the older boy, applied pressure as he spun and broke the bone in the challenger's forearm. Jim Casey was a good teacher and Roger and Bobby were smart and willing students. Jim also worked with Danno O'Mahoney's young son 'Punchy' for a time. 'Punchy' showed some promise, having inherited his father's skill

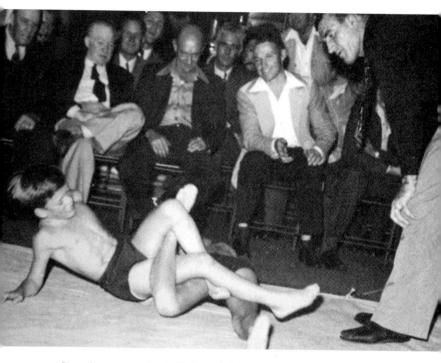

Roger Sampson applies the 'flying toehold' on Bobby Lundeen. Jim Casey referees. The crowd always enjoyed these exhibitions.

but Jim could not work with him long enough to bring it out fully. We will hear more of Jim's involvement with the training of young boys in athletics a little later on.

When Jim resumed wrestling in California, he did so with a bang. He was booked for matches in Los Angeles, San Francisco, San Diego and in the states of Washington and Oregon. He fought as many as three matches a week and won consistently. Now he was getting top billing and top money.

In 1944, Jim won two very significant heavyweight championship titles. One was the Canadian Championship and the other the Pedro Brazil in Rio de Janiero for the South American Crown. By then, he was generally considered by everyone in the wrestling game to be the West Coast Heavyweight Champion and by many to be the US Champion.

In 1945, Jim's brother Steve moved out to California. Not wanting to be overshadowed again by his brother, Jim moved on – this time to Houston, Texas. From there, he appeared in matches all over the Gulf Coast as well as in Dallas, Fort Worth and San Antonio. Again, he was given top billing at all his matches.

It was during a match in 1945 in Galveston, Texas, that Jim met the woman who was to become his wife. He met her in a manner befitting a film script. Jim was thrown out of the ring by his opponent that night and was sent crashing into three people seated in the front row. They were a Mr and Mrs Dougherty and a young lady named Myrtle Gillmore, who worked for Mr Dougherty. All 240 pounds of Jim came hurtling at them, knocking them to the floor and causing back injuries to both Mr Dougherty and Myrtle Gillmore. After the match, Jim sought them out to check on their condition and so they underwent a second, more proper, introduction.

The following Monday, Myrtle was called upon to work as a substitute cashier at the Isle cinema and who should appear in search of a ticket but big Jim Casey. The rest is history. They were married in San Francisco in January 1946, with Steve as their best man. Apparently, a violent collision at the start of a relationship is no detriment to a happy marriage. Jim and Myrtle were married for fifty-four years and raised three children.

Jim Casey wearing his Pacific Coast Heavyweight Championship belt.

Now we must address the situation that we spoke of earlier, in which Jim Casey might possibly have been named the World Heavyweight Wrestling Champion.

Jim Jeffries, a boxer who had won the World Heavyweight Boxing Championship from Bob Fitzsimmons in 1899 and who retired undefeated in 1905, owned an arena in Burbank, California, that he called Jim Jeffries' Barn. In this arena, Jeffries sponsored a unique wrestling tournament. To qualify, a wrestler had to appear in at least one match each year for three years. This was a single elimination tournament. Once beaten, you were out of the running. At the end of the three years, two finalists would emerge and meet in a match to determine the champion.

Jim Casey emerged unbeaten from his three years of competition. As luck would have it, the other finalist was none other than Jim's good friend Danno O'Mahoney. Danno had spent two or three years in the US Army but came back home to resume his wrestling career. It is interesting to note that, in the course of the elimination tournament, such supposedly great wrestlers as Jim Londos, Frank Sexton and Sandor Szabo all backed out of scheduled matches with Jim Casey. I can't imagine a greater compliment to any wrestler than to have these 'champions' refuse to meet him.

When they met in the final match, Jim was able to beat Danno, his close friend and the former World Heavyweight Champion, in two straight falls. Jim used a 'go-behind' toehold that his brother Paddy had taught him. When this hold is properly applied struggling is useless. In fact, too much struggling will inevitably result in a broken ankle.

Weeshie Fogarty pictured with Jim Casey's wife Myrtle at Jim's grave in Texas.

This tournament win meant Jim was eligible to meet the World Heavyweight Champion to wrestle for his title. That champion was, of course, Jim's brother, Steve 'Crusher' Casey. This was a unique situation, to say the least. The two brothers talked it over at length and finally concluded that it just wouldn't be right to have two brothers squaring off in the ring and so, Jim graciously passed up the opportunity to wear the championship belt himself. One has to remark on the situation which now prevailed: Steve Casey was the World Champion and Jim Casey was the acknowledged best challenger, thus, they had to be adjudged the number one and number two heavyweight wrestlers in the world.

Apparently, the promoters and, in particular, Paul Bowser who exerted a great deal of influence in those days, didn't think so. When Steve injured his back and had to vacate his title temporarily, Jim was the logical man to be named to succeed him as champion but Paul Bowser didn't like Jim and perhaps the following episode explains why.

Some months earlier, Bowser had set up a match for Steve with a wrestler named Manuel Cortez. It appears that both Cortez and Bowser had somehow got the mistaken impression that Steve was going to 'carry' Cortez through the match – to go easy on him. When they discovered shortly before the match that Steve had no such intention, Cortez refused to come out of his dressing room and into the ring.

Jim Casey, at ringside, asked his brother what was going on and Steve said, 'I don't know. I guess maybe the guy's afraid of me.'

With that, Jim sprang into the ring, grabbed the microphone from the MC and began to taunt the challenger. 'What's going on here? Where is Cortez? I saw him in the

dressing room. Why won't he come out? Is he scared of my brother or what?'

That bout was cancelled when Cortez vanished and Jim earned himself a black mark in Paul Bowser's book.

(*opposite*) Jim Casey with two of his trophies. The silver cup (*right*) was presented to Jim, Tom and Steve Casey by Leverette Saltonstall, Governor of Massachusetts, the same day Jim set a new 2,000-metre rowing record (6.35) on the Charles River, Boston, in 1940. The Jim Jeffries Trophy (*left*) commemorates the former world heavyweight boxing champion. Jeffries won the title in 1899 and also had a great passion for wrestling – he used it to train for his boxing bouts.

SEVENTEEN

THE FURTHER ADVENTURES OF
JIM CASEY

Undaunted, Jim continued his wrestling career but the wrestling game was beginning to change and not for the better. Toward the end of the 1940s, wrestling was fast becoming an aspect of 'show business' rather than a sport. Showmanship, gimmicks, mock rivalries, tag-team matches, 'good guys and bad guys', outrageous costumes and ridiculous names began to become the mainstay of what had once been a challenging sport.

During this period, Jim Casey wrestled one of the first of the 'showmen' of the wrestling ring. He was 'Gorgeous George' Wagner, perhaps the best known of the 'show biz' wrestlers. With long platinum blond locks, a lavish robe of figured silk and a valet who preceded him into the ring spraying perfume, 'Gorgeous George' appealed to the many women who were devotees of the sport, both at the arenas and watching at home.

'Gorgeous George' was a good wrestler and a very strong one but what Jim Casey did to him in their match can be seen in the photograph (*next page*) where Jim seems to have messed up those 'gorgeous' blond locks somewhat.

Jim Casey introduces 'Gorgeous George' to some of the finer points of wrestling. Gorgeous George, whose real name was George Raymond Wagner was born in Butte, Nebraska, in 1915. He died in 1963.

This match was one of the most memorable matches in his long career. Another outstanding match was with a man named George 'K.O.' Koverly. In the early 1940s, when Steve was still champion and Jim was winning consistently, this Koverly fellow got it into his head that he could beat them, or at least, that's what he said and believed. He had met an Irish man in the wrestling ring called Dr Pat O'Callaghan. He was an Olympic champion weight-thrower from Cork who had come to America to wrestle. His last match was with George Koverly who beat him so badly that he gave up wrestling forever and went back home to Ireland. After this win, Koverly began to brag that he was going to 'put all the Irishmen to sleep'. This pointed reference was undoubtedly meant for the Caseys, the most prominent Irishmen in the game at the time. When Jim heard of this boast, he went after 'K.O.' Koverly with a vengeance and would not rest until he had arranged a match with him. The match finally took place in California and Jim Casey gave Koverly a trouncing he would never forget. Jim put a wristlock on Koverly, followed with a side-arm lock, spun him and slammed him to the canvas with a thud that could be heard out in the street. There was absolutely no way for Koverly to break the hold unless he was willing to break his arm. 'K.O.' wasn't willing to do that so he meekly gave up, signalling to the referee that he was through. The photograph of the match gives some indication of the pain and humiliation that Jim caused this upstart who was going to put all the Irishmen 'to sleep'.

Jim had another memorable bout in Galveston, Texas, in December 1947 but this was a boxing match. Jim had met a wrestler named Karl Davis in a wrestling match the week

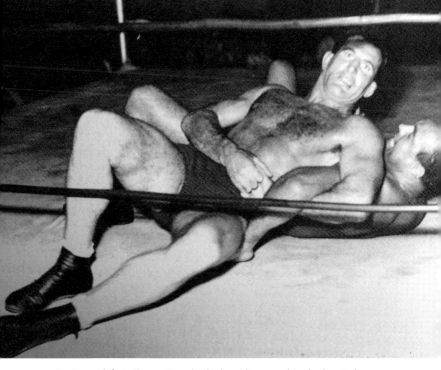

Jim Casey defeats George Koverly, the legendary wrestler who boasted
that he 'would put all Irish wrestlers to sleep'.

before. Davis was a professional boxer turned wrestler but in
his bout against Jim, he soon discovered that his wrestling
skills were no match for the rugged Irishman, so he reverted
to boxing, openly slugging Jim about the head and body. At
the conclusion of the match, an understandably upset Jim
challenged Davis to a rematch – whether in wrestling or
boxing. Davis accepted and they met a week later in the
boxing ring in the Galveston Auditorium.

Myrtle Casey had made Jim a beautiful robe which he wore going into the ring. He wore it on this particular night but he discovered to his surprise and amusement of the crowd, that he could not pull off the robe due to the bulky boxing gloves he wore. Of course, a wrestler's robe made no allowance for gloves. The start of the match was delayed while Jim took off his gloves so that his robe could be removed. Karl Davis joined the crowd in laughing at his minor predicament but he didn't laugh for long. Though he was a former boxer going against a wrestler, he soon found that he had his work cut out for him. Jim boxed him for five rounds, noticing almost immediately the nervousness and fear in his opponent's eyes.

Jim Casey packed a terrific punch in a fist that had to travel only a few inches to have a devastating effect. He admits to having used such a punch to very good advantage in some wrestling matches when his opponent began slugging. Jim was confident from the first round that he could beat Davis easily but he wanted the crowd to get its money's worth. Five rounds were plenty, he thought, so in the sixth round, he dropped Davis to the canvas with one lightning punch. No one ever challenged him to a boxing match again.

It was in this same period that Jim had a strange and unsettling experience. Driving into Dallas one evening to appear in a match, the headlights on his car inexplicably went out. Unable to drive, he pulled onto the shoulder of the road and flagged down a police car. The policemen recognised him instantly and provided a lighted escort for him, driving his darkened car, to the arena in time for his match.

After the match, Jim showered and dressed and then began to wonder how he was going to get back to his hotel.

At that moment, a strange man appeared outside his dressing-room door, eager to meet the great Jim Casey. He was a short, stocky fellow in a heavy black overcoat and grey snap-brim fedora.

'You don't know me, Jim,' he said, 'but you knew my ex-wife and my two kids out in San Francisco. She was working at the Hotel Arnoux where you were staying. She's told me that you were real nice to her and to my little boy and girl. She said you were like a second daddy to them.

'She told me you used to give my boy and a lot of other kids around there wrestling lessons right there on the carpet in the hotel lobby. Anyhow, I wanted to meet you and shake your hand. Can I give you a lift somewhere?'

So Jim gratefully accepted the offer. On their way through Dallas the stranger suggested they stop for a drink. Jim being agreeable, the fellow pulled to the curb in front of a darkened nightclub. 'This is my place,' he said.

'Why isn't it open at this time of night?' asked Jim.

'Oh, I had a little trouble and got closed up,' he said, 'but I will be back in business soon.'

The fellow went about flipping on light switches and then got them a drink. Jim had a beer; the fellow poured himself a shot. He walked to the jukebox and dropped in a few coins. In a minute, music was blaring out of the neon-lit Wurlitzer.

Suddenly, the stranger whirled and pulled a gun from his pocket that he aimed at the jukebox. 'Damned thing's too loud.' He muttered, as he began pumping bullets into it. As the sparks flew and the music abruptly stopped, Jim grabbed the strange little man and threw him to the floor. He pinned his gun hand to the floor with his foot, then took the gun away from him.

'Don't hurt me, Casey, don't hurt me,' he implored.

'What the hell's the matter with you? Are you nuts?' asked Jim.

'I'm sorry. I don't know what got into me. Just don't hurt me, please, Casey.'

So Jim got him up off the floor, out of the nightclub and into his car. They drove then to Jim's hotel, with Jim reading him the riot act all the way. When they arrived at the hotel, Jim emptied the gun of its one remaining bullet and tossed it back into the car.

The next time he saw that man was on a Sunday morning in November 1963 when he saw him on television. The cameras were focused that morning on the basement of the Dallas police station, from which the accused murderer Lee Harvey Oswald was to be transferred.

Jim and Myrtle, by then living near Houston, Texas, watched as Oswald was borne along a concrete walkway by a squad of burly lawmen. Suddenly, one of the onlookers stepped forward from the crowd and fired a pistol point-blank into Oswald's body.

Jim stared in disbelief, sprang to his feet and pointing to the screen, he shouted to his wife, 'That's the crazy guy who shot up the jukebox years ago in his Dallas nightclub. That's the same guy, I know it, that's Jack Ruby.'

Some time later, the rest of the world was informed by television newscasters: Lee Harvey Oswald's murderer had indeed been Jack Ruby.

Let us return now to the continuance of Jim Casey's wrestling career. In 1947, Jim went back to Ireland on a short holiday. He stopped off in London where he attended a wrestling match in an arena. He was not there for pleasure; he had business to conduct, which he did in the usual unorthodox Casey manner. Entering the ring, he took the microphone from the MC and issued a challenge to wrestle anyone who would care to take him on. In particular, he challenged Bert Assirati, then the British Heavyweight Champion. A promoter named Sammy King came to the fore at this point and began to make arrangements for this championship match. He arranged for Assirati and his entourage to meet with Jim and his attorney to sign the necessary papers. Assirati never showed up and continued to dodge Jim for days thereafter. Some time later, Assirati was signed to meet another challenger in the same arena.

On the night of the match, Jim Casey entered the arena and, just before the main event was announced, leaped into the ring, grabbed the microphone – again – and began to taunt and berate the champion. He yelled that Assirati was afraid of him and that he had ducked out on the signing and would fight only handpicked opponents. With that, Jim shrugged off his overcoat, revealing that he was wearing his wrestling trunks and was ready to go at the mat. He started toward Assirati's corner. 'Come on, come on, it's time to put up or shut up. Or are you afraid of me?'

But he was talking to an empty corner and a vacant stool. Assirati had flown the coop.

Upon Assirati's departure, Jim laid claim, by default, to the Heavyweight Wrestling championship of England. He received a great deal of support for his claim in England and in the United States as well.

After his return to America, Jim and Myrtle moved to California for a while, living first in San Leandro and then in Oakland. Jim continued wrestling and winning consistently.

'Crusher' Casey's Bar, 340 Massachusetts Avenue, Boston.

In 1949, they bought a Vagabond house trailer and drove it
back to Boston. The trip was a real hair-raiser: climbing
through steep icy mountain passes and experiencing brake
failure on steep downgrades were but a couple of the high-
lights.

Once safely back in Boston, Jim entered into a business
partnership with his brother Steve. They opened a bar called
Crusher Casey's directly across the street from the Boston
Arena where both brothers had often wrestled. Their brother
Tom came in with them for a while but then decided to go
into business for himself. He bought and operated a bar in
Charlestown, Massachusetts.

Jim continued to book a few matches in the Boston area.
He was still well known and was acknowledged as one of the

few remaining 'scientific' wrestlers, so he always packed the house.

Nonetheless, Jim was unable to get a match with Frank Sexton, the 'declared' champion, who was managed by Paul Bowser, the promoter who essentially ran the wrestling game in the northeastern part of the country. Sexton didn't want to meet Jim – earlier he had ducked out of the match with him in the Jim Jeffries tournament in California – and Paul Bowser didn't want to take a chance on relinquishing the championship. In his anger and frustration, Jim had a loud confrontation with Bowser, which did him no good at all.

One night, Jim was booked into an arena in Holyoke, Massachusetts, to wrestle a man named Gunnar Barlund. After Jim had dressed for the match, a man named Burbank, who was Bowser's Holyoke connection, came in and told Jim that there had been a substitution. Instead of Gunnar Barlund, Jim was expected to wrestle a man named Silverstein, the Heavyweight Champion of the 1936 Olympics and considered by many to be the best wrestler then working. It was a classic double-cross. Paul Bowser obviously wanted Silverstein to 'fix' Jim Casey once and for all. He wanted to teach Jim to stay in his subservient place. He obviously didn't know Jim as well as he thought he did.

When Burbank told Jim of the switch, Jim flew into a rage. 'Where is he?' he bellowed. 'Get him out here. I'll kill him. He'll never see my back at all. Get him out here – he can't beat me. I'll tear his guts out. He can't beat me; nobody in the country can beat me.'

Burbank rushed off to tell Silverstein what Silverstein had probably already heard through the thin dressing-room walls but whether he heard it directly or indirectly, it had a dramatic effect on him. He very prudently decided to remain

Between falls –
Jim Casey

'Mighty' Jim Casey as he waits in the ring for an opponent who refused
to finish the match.

in his dressing room and not risk a confrontation in the ring
with this red-hot, raging Irishman. So much for Paul Bowser's
attempt to 'fix' Jim Casey.

EIGHTEEN

LIFE AFTER WRESTLING

After his superb wrestling career ended, Jim Casey opened a bar in Cambridge, Massachusetts, near Harvard Square, which he named 'Casey's Main Event'. His wife was by his side. The business was an instant success, for the Casey name continued to be a drawing card and they had made many friends in the area.

Jim and Myrtle, thinking to put down roots in the Boston area, purchased an imposing Victorian style home in Dorchester, a small mansion built at the turn of the century by the Boston City Architect A.H. Vinal. They invested thousands of dollars and hundreds of hours of hard work on the home and its grounds, with the result that the home became a local showplace. It was so lovely that it was featured in the Hollywood film *Summer Solstice*, starring Henry Fonda and Myrna Loy. The stained glass windows were the envy of every antique dealer in the northeast and Jim and Myrtle refused many offers from them. Jim did a great deal of the restoration himself, including the removal and replacement of a huge brick chimney and the flues of the four fireplaces the house contained. Local stonemasons predicted disaster when they learned what Jim planned to do and said it couldn't be done. They obviously didn't know Jim Casey.

The house had three bedrooms, a nursery, a music room (with both an organ and a grand piano), a huge living and dining room, a restaurant-sized kitchen and pantry and a grand entrance hall, which was graced with bas-reliefs of Trojan horses in classical Greek style. The enormous chandeliers contained thousands of sparkling teardrop Waterford crystals.

While still operating Casey's Main Event, Jim and Myrtle developed greater ambitions and decided to open a first class supper club in the area that would offer dining, dancing and a variety of floorshows and special events. They leased and completely renovated an old theatre building, which was a very expensive undertaking indeed. However, the work and expense were worth it for, when they had finished, they had created one of the finest nightclubs in the Boston area. Named the 318 Club, it featured fine cuisine, a pleasant and relaxing décor and dancing to a variety of bands. Special events were staged frequently: amateur nights, polka nights, Irish nights, waltz contests and so on. A dress code was rigidly adhered to and an old friend of theirs named Bill Greene was stationed at the entrance to the club to enforce it and to keep out any undesirable characters.

Indeed, there were plenty of undesirables to be kept out of the club. There were several mobs of gangsters operating in the Boston area in those days and they tried to 'muscle in' on honest businessmen where they could.

Jim's first experience with the mob came just after the completion of the remodelling of the theatre. There had been two old juke boxes left in the building when Jim and Myrtle took over (there had been an earlier attempt to make the old theatre into a club – its character can be deduced from its name: The Bucket of Blood). At any rate, Jim had tossed the battered old boxes into the alley. Soon after, Jim was paid a visit by two unsavoury looking characters who told Jim that they had a contract for supplying records for those machines and that the contract was still in force, therefore Jim had better get them back into the building and start paying them for the privilege or there would be trouble. Jim promptly sent them packing, with the hoodlums protesting all the while that there would be serious trouble over this.

A few days later, while Jim was upstairs in the club talking with his accountant, a tough-looking man in a snap-brim hat showed up and told Jim that he was now in big trouble, for he was the 'strong arm guy' from the mob and he was going to force Jim to cooperate.

Jim promptly flattened the mobster with one punch and, while he was lying senseless on the floor, he stripped him of his gun and tossed it across the room. He stood the poor fellow up and put an arm lock on him that kept him doubled over from the waist. He hustled him down the stairs, through the foyer and out the front door. A heavy fall of snow had been ploughed from the street, resulting in huge snow banks that nearly covered the footpaths. Still holding the man in an arm lock, Jim rushed him out the door and threw him headlong into the bank of snow. Later, Jim threw the gun off a bridge into the Charles River.

Though Jim and Myrtle received threatening phone calls both at the club and at their home, members of that particular gang never again visited the Caseys. There was another cheap mobster, however, who had his eye on the 318 Club. He wanted to use it as a hangout for himself and his mob members and perhaps was also anxious to take over some of the club's 'action' for himself. His name was Buddy McLean

A political banquet at the Casey 318 Lounge in Somerville, Massachusetts. Jim Casey is standing to the left of the photograph.

and he and his gang were perhaps the most notorious characters in the Somerville area.

One night a bartender informed Jim that three of McLean's men were inside the club and he was afraid of what might happen. They were the Sacramone brothers, along with another 'tough guy'. When he saw them, Jim flew into a rage. He grabbed one by the scuff of the neck and began to escort him unceremoniously to the front door. The other two followed, bellowing at Jim. A local policeman was on duty in the club and he came up, huffing and puffing, and saying 'I'll do it, I'll do it.' His real concern seemed to be that no harm was to come to the mobsters.

Jim reached the foyer and turned to confront the two thugs, still holding the third by the back of the neck. Not knowing whether they had guns, Jim knew he had to take them out of action quickly. So he threw the man he was holding into the other two, knocking all three to the floor. At this point, the doorman Bill Greene jumped in to help Jim out. Between them, they managed to get the three men subdued, checked for guns (they were relieved to find none) and kicked them out into the street.

It soon became the talk of the town that Buddy McLean was going to get even with Jim and was going to 'get a piece of' the 318 Club. He made a number of threatening phone calls to try to scare Jim. Jim's reply: 'You'd better bring an army if you want to try to beat me.'

Jim and Myrtle operated the 318 Club for about a year and a half, after which they sold up. It may be that they had settled on the wrong area in which to open such a high-class nightclub. Not too many years later, that same area became involved in a violent gang war in which the final tally – of

Jim and Myrtle Casey with their children, *(l–r)*: Steve, Patricia and James.

known dead – reached forty. The gangs that were systematically wiping each other out were those of one George McLaughlin and Jim's old nemesis Buddy McLean.

Buddy McLean was one of the victims of this gang warfare, as was George McLaughlin. Ironically, perhaps, McLean was gunned down directly across the street from the 318 Club and it is thought that he had just come from the club and was heading for his car. Americo Sacramone, one of the toughs whom Jim had thrown out of the club, was with McLean and was seriously wounded by the same shotgun-wielding assailant who shot down his boss.

NINETEEN

THE CASEYS AND THE KIDS

It is a pleasure now to tell of the wonderful work that Jim and Myrtle Casey did with the neighbourhood kids in Dorchester.

I have alluded several times in the course of this account to Jim Casey's affection for children. Throughout his life, Jim had been a modern day Pied Piper, drawing children to him in droves. All of the Caseys share the enviable trait of being warm and likable: they all made legions of friends wherever they went. Jim Casey had a particular appeal to children, especially to young boys who admired him, not just for his strength or the fame of his name, but for his interest in their welfare and the willingness to invest his time in training and rehabilitating juvenile delinquents into wholesome boys as eager to follow his example in living the life of a good, productive citizen, as they were to learn from him the basic fundamentals of wrestling, rowing and baseball.

Baseball? That's hardly a sport that Jim Casey excelled in, or had even played, but coach baseball he did and predictably, formed a team of champions.

Jim gathered all the young lads in his local Catholic parish and devoted hours on end to their physical development and training. In the summer, he took them to the river and taught

Jim Casey coaching his
youthful baseball team.

them to row; in winter, he took them to the gym and taught them to wrestle. In every season, he taught them honesty, morality, good sportsmanship and personal integrity, both by his words and by his example. His wife Myrtle shared his life long affection and concern for these underprivileged children and joined him in this work.

As to the baseball: here again we have a case of a Casey taking matters into his own hands when they see an injustice being done. As most parents of young boys know (in America, at least), many Little League groups are poorly run and are dominated by adults who have lost sight of the principal objective of the group's existence, which is to encourage and facilitate the playing of baseball. Rather, these adults use the organisation for their own designs, for the furtherance of their own child's ambitions (or their ambition for the child) at the expense of others. So it was in Dorchester in those days.

When their son Jimmy was of playing age, Jim and Myrtle refused to turn his fate over to the selfish aims of the local Little League group. They realised that there were a couple of dozen other young boys who, for one reason or another, had been excluded from the exclusive clubs that the misguided adults had formed.

What to do? Never at a loss for long for solutions, Jim and Myrtle Casey formed a baseball team of their own, called 'Casey's All-Stars'. They paid for all the gloves, bats and equipment from their own pockets and Myrtle made them uniforms. Jim took a crash course in baseball (mostly from Myrtle) and began working on the basic skills with the boys. What Jim didn't know about baseball, he made up for in his insistence on arduous physical training and the development

Patricia (team mascot), Jim and Myrtle Casey stand behind their Casey's All-Stars. (No, that is <u>not</u> a Casey at the bat.)

of self-discipline. When describing those days, Jim invariably referred to a bat as a 'club'.

Jim and Myrtle fashioned a pretty fair country ball club from these cast-offs and misfits. They challenged other Little League teams and won every game they played. Jimmy Casey turned out to be a very talented pitcher, who won every game he pitched. The boys played well under Jim's tutelage – and **play** is the operative word here. Jim sent his boys out to **play** the game of baseball; he had no base coaches but let the boys play the game freely.

Soon, Casey's All-Stars became the talk of Boston. The stands were packed for every game and local sports writers came to watch and to write glowing accounts of this pickup team and their famous wrestler coach. Some games were even attended by scouts from the Boston Red Sox.

As if wrestling, rowing and baseball were not enough to keep the boys occupied, Jim also took them on frequent hunting trips with his pack of specially trained hunting dogs. With the help of his hunting partner Gil Martin, Jim had converted a delivery van into a rudimentary camper with bunks attached to the inside walls and a heater and a cooking stove welded to the frame. In this makeshift mobile home, he would take dozen or so of the neighbourhood boys into the New England woods – to Maine, Vermont or New Hampshire. They would make camp and then go off on glorious night-time raccoon hunts, the hounds joyously baying on the trail of a racoon, the boys crashing through the underbrush of the woods in hot pursuit. Myrtle describes their typical return from three or four days and nights in the woods with her eyes glistening fondly at the recollection: 'Jim would pull up to the curb and motion for me to come over and look. In the back of the van would be a wild tangle of sleeping boys and dogs, with a dog here sleeping with its head on a boy's back and here a dog's rear end sticking up between two equally exhausted boys. They were dirty and pretty ripe but they would all be sleeping with happy grins on their faces.'

All the Casey brothers shared a life long interest in hunting, stemming, most likely, from their boyhood days in Ballaugh when they joyously followed their dogs on the track of a scampering hare, cradling their father's faulty old shotgun as they ran. In particular, they were devoted to the training of hunting dogs, a pursuit which was not only enjoyable for the pure sport of it but in which one could compete by entering dogs in field trials, competing against the dogs of other men – and yes, the Casey brothers did love to compete.

When Jim Casey described a hunt, his love and admiration for his dogs shone through. In describing their exploits, he spoke glowingly of their native intelligence and their trainability. In particular, he mentioned Ginger, a crossbreed of Walker Hound and Red Bone whom he described as being 'unbeatable'. Indeed, Ginger won the grade class night hunt in Freeport, Maine, against a large field of championship grade hounds. Ginger was a 'two way' dog, who hunted raccoons by night and squirrels by day – the techniques employed were quite different for each animal. Incredible as it may seem, Jim was once offered $40,000 for Ginger. This was in the 1950s, when $40,000 was worth considerably more than it is today. Little Red, another of Jim's favourites, was a Red Bone hound that joined Ginger in hunting raccoons at night and was unbeatable at hunting bobcat in the daytime. Jim described, in vivid terms, the ability of these two dogs to track a raccoon unerringly until, in desperation, it scrambled high into the upper branches of a tree. Their baying would bring the hunters to their location, where they would patiently 'mark' the tree by standing with their forepaws on the trunk of the tree until the raccoon was shot down out of its branches.

Jim also talked lovingly of two dogs that were trained to hunt black bear. He spoke with disdain of those hunters who turn loose packs of dogs to pursue this dangerous creature: a pack milling about a black bear will stumble over one another and a fallen dog is easy prey to the open paw of a bear, with its fearsome claws. Jim knew that to bring a bear to the point where he is driven to climb a tree and is thus vulnerable to

Jim Casey with five of his favourite hunting dogs: Hudson, Lady, Ginger, Jack and Ranger.

the hunter's gun, only two dogs – two well-trained dogs – are needed. These two dogs, working together, can harry a bear for hours until he becomes exhausted. They do this by taking turns nipping at the bear's hindquarters. When the bear turns to fend off one snapping dog, he exposes his hindquarters to the second dog, which takes his turn nipping at the enraged bear. Good dogs can carry on this harassment for hours, narrowly avoiding the slashing paws of the enraged bear. Jim had two of the finest bear dogs in those days: Jack, a Walker and Plot Hound combination, and Ranger, a Black and Tan breed. Jim's eyes glowed brightly when he described the exploits of these dogs, as they did when he described the achievements of the children that he and Myrtle had taken under their wings.

Jim's life-long interest in dogs was to be the medium through which he would become involved with America's space shuttle astronauts.

However, in those days in Dorchester, his interest in dogs was coupled with his interest in kids. I'm sure there are many grown men today whose lives were touched, and forever changed, by the love and concern and direction given them by this rough, tough, champion Irish wrestler and his equally caring and loving wife. One can only hope that some of the adults running the Dorchester Little League programme were able to profit from their example as well.

As for Jim and Myrtle's own boys: it seems that Jimmy and Stevie had obviously inherited those marvellous Casey genes that made for superb athletes and, I might add, their mother's. Myrtle Casey was a superb softball player and bowler (a good enough bowler to have appeared in televised championship matches), so inheriting her genes couldn't have hurt either. At any rate, these two boys, rowing for the

Jim Casey and his son Steve admire a black bear, silver racoon and a trophy deer from a fruitful hunting trip.

Riverside Boat Club, won the Boys' Doubles event in the New England Junior rowing Championships in 1961. This was over a half mile course and Jimmy, who was fourteen, and Stevie, who was twelve and a half, easily beat the other two finalists – two boys from a crack team from the New York Athletic Club, considered by many to be the best club in all of New England. So the Casey tradition for winning lives on in Jim Casey's children and in his brothers' children as well.

In the late summer of 1963, Jim and Myrtle decided to return to California to examine the business opportunities that might be available there but they never made it. Stopping off at Myrtle's family home in Galveston, Texas, Jim became

Jim Casey *(on the left)* teaching a crew to row, *(l–r)*: James Casey, Charles Fitzgerald, Eddie Courtney and Steve Casey.

aware of the potential profit to be made in real estate there; the entire Texas Gulf Coast, he could see, was ripe for a dramatic economic upturn. His good friend Cecil Wells was instrumental in persuading Jim to stay and to try his hand at the real estate business. So Jim and Myrtle settled down in Alta Loma, a small town between Houston and Galveston.

We will leave them for now with Jim and Myrtle buying and selling real estate and opening a kennel, about which more will be said later. For now, let us go on to recount the further adventures of the rest of the Casey clan. They, too, were so active that it is difficult to tell a comprehensive story unless we consider them one by one through the years as we have done with Jim.

TWENTY

STEVE

In resuming the account of the career of older brother Steve 'Crusher' Casey, it is well to reflect back upon the scene of his triumphant return to Ireland after winning the World Heavyweight Championship in 1938. You will recall that it was at the conclusion of this visit that Steve returned to America with younger brothers Tom and Jim in tow.

To describe his return to Ireland as triumphant is no overstatement. A few excerpts from the *Cork Examiner* for 20 August 1938 bear this out:

> Wherever Casey went in Cork on Tuesday, he was fol-
> lowed by large crowds. When he visited the office of the
> 'Examiner' large crowds followed him and the same story
> was to be told at the Victoria Hotel and the City Hall.'

Concerning his return to Sneem:

> The little village of Sneem, in the shadows of Dunkerrin
> Mountain, was tonight ablaze with bonfires and bright
> with flags and bunting when Steve Casey arrived from
> Cork for his holiday in his native place. 'Sneem is proud
> of her champion' read banners hung across the street and

every man and woman in Sneem and the surrounding districts seemed to be present to welcome Steve despite the inclement weather.

On the way from Cork, the champion received ovations in Macroom, Kenmare and Parknasilla, but the heartiest and most enthusiastic of all awaited him at the outskirts of Sneem, where a guard of honour of horsemen and cyclists led a large crowd towards the car which brought Casey home. People surged round him to shake his hand.

Steve, however, didn't spend much time basking in triumph. For this holiday in Ireland was to be something of a 'busman's holiday' for him. A match had been arranged for him on 26 August in Dublin against none other than the ex-champion Danno O'Mahoney, the man who was to become such great friends with Jim Casey in America three years later.

Danno, from Ballydehob, County Cork, was a formidable wrestler. He had developed a wrestling throw, the name of which became Danno's nickname thereafter, the 'Irish Whip'. It has been said that Steve Casey's own 'Killarney Flip' was a variation of the 'Irish Whip' and that he had Danno to thank for it. Be that as it may, Steve met Danno, who was trying to regain his world championship, in a twenty-round match on that August night in Dublin. That match ended in a draw but the two met again on 18 September in Cork. Here's a newspaper account written by an eyewitness:

What ensued was probably the greatest fight in wrestling history and it took place here in Ireland at the Mallow Racecourse. It was not just Danno and Steve. It was the whole O'Mahoney clan of Ballydehob versus the Caseys of Sneem.

… It was a twenty round contest and only in the closing seconds of the twentieth round did Steve beat the great Danno who had invented the 'Irish Whip' that had made him champion and which kept him there and who was now himself beaten by his own throw laid on Casey.

Danno O'Mahoney's life came to a tragic end in 1950, when he was fatally injured in a road collision. Years later, while Steve was visiting Ireland, he and his brothers, Jack and Paddy, made a touching visit to honour the O'Mahoney clan in Ballydehob and to be honoured by them in return. In October 1985, Steve, Paddy and Jack gathered at a pub in Ballydehob named 'The Irish Whip' in Danno's honour to meet with the three surviving O'Mahoney brothers, Will, Dermott and Jack. Again to quote from newspaper coverage of this touching event: 'The Casey brothers spoke with great affection of Danno. Steve said, "We all lost a great friend when Danno died and more especially me." The meeting was at times emotional as they recalled old memories and it was very evident that both the O'Mahoneys and Caseys had great respect for each other's families and their meeting marked an unforgettable experience long to be remembered by them and strengthen with affection their bond of friendship.'

Steve's exploits also became the subject of a hit record: 'Steve Casey from Sneem' – a catchy tune with lyrics praising the 'Crusher' from County Kerry was recorded by Gerry Burns and could be heard playing from every radio and jukebox throughout Ireland in 1938.

After his return to the United States, Steve resumed taking on all comers in wrestling (and beating them), as we have already reported and, like his brother Jim, he also tried his hand at boxing. Again we quote from a newspaper account told in retrospect by Dermot C. Clarke, a sports journalist of the day: 'Unable to find anyone to beat him at wrestling, Steve wondered about the result of matching wrestlers against boxers. He challenged Tiger Warrentown, the heavyweight, to fight him in Boston. So easily did Casey win that all who saw the fight, including Jack Dempsey, were of the belief that Steve would beat Joe Louis, the then Heavyweight Boxing Champion. Louis did not want to know about it even though Steve offered $50,000 (at the 1940s value). It was the only fight that Joe Louis ever refused.' Can there be a greater compliment paid than this, that one of the greatest boxing champions the world had ever seen refused to fight him – he who was not even a boxer but a champion wrestler. What a fearsome man he must have been.

Steve's toughness was graphically illustrated some years later when he survived an experience that surely would have killed a lesser man.

In January 1968, while Steve was closing up his bar in Boston for the night, three armed men entered, intent upon robbery. Panicking, the three young thugs began shooting, killing a patron who had lingered to talk to Steve. Steve was shot three times and he was rushed, near death, to a local hospital. Two of the bullets had lodged just below his heart and these the doctors removed. Another, which had lodged in his back, was judged too dangerous to probe for and so remained in his back for the rest of his life. His recovery from this deadly assault amazed doctors, who marvelled at the strength, stamina, and recuperative powers of this fifty-nine-year-old Irishman – but they didn't know the Caseys. The three would-be thieves were rounded up by the police, tried, convicted and sentenced to life imprisonment.

Steve had married Mary Rogers in 1948 and fathered two sons, Paddy and Mike, and a daughter, Margaret. Paddy and Mike, like Jim's two boys, proved to be solid chips off the proverbial Casey block.

Steve Casey had opened a rowing club near his home in Cohassett, Massachusetts, and there his boys learned rowing from one of the best oarsmen in the world, their father. In 1970, Paddy and Mike went to Ireland on a holiday with their father Steve. As it happened, they arrived just before the Castletownbere rowing regatta where, in 1934, the Caseys had beaten the vaunted Whiddy Crew. Paddy and Mike joined forces with Patrick and Steve Casey, their Uncle Paddy's boys, and entered the four-oar gig race. Steve's boys were not familiar with this type of boat, for it was not used in Boston where they raced. Nonetheless, they were game and entered the race with their cousins. They were short a coxswain, so Paddy Casey took on the job, although he was far heavier, of course, than the usual coxswain.

At the start of the race, the young Casey cousins pulled out to a three-length lead. They had been told (erroneously and perhaps intentionally) that they had to row out beyond two buoys and then return. With their three-length lead, they passed the first buoy and sprinted on toward the second. It was then that they saw the other boats turning at the first buoy and heading back to the starting line.

Realising that a mistake had been made, Paddy's boy Steve shouted to the crew and made them turn for home. By then,

A younger generation of Caseys after winning a coveted four-oar gig race at Castletownbere in 1970, *(l–r)*: Steve's sons Mike and Paddy, and Paddy's sons Patrick and Steve.

their three-length lead had vanished and instead they found themselves ten lengths behind. Dismayed but not discouraged, the four boys put their backs and shoulders into it and rapidly caught up with the other boats. With a superhuman surge, the boys flew by the other four-oared boats and crossed the finish line first by a nose.

'Crusher' Casey was pretty nonchalant about the whole thing when interviewed after the race. After all, this kind of performance, which might be judged incredible if done by any other athletes, was the norm by which the Caseys judged themselves.

'I thought our lads would be too raw to beat the experience of the Castletownbere boys,' he said. 'But they did a good job. Yes, I am happy and proud to see them win. In my day, we always rowed to win too. It's good to see the young fellows have the same will.' And, he might have added, the same Casey genes that make superhuman effort and achievement seem commonplace.

Steve Casey was a guest of honour (or 'roastee') at a dinner in Hull where 240 of his friends and colleagues met to 'roast and toast' him. Jim had come back to Boston for the occasion and had a few words to say about his oldest brother. So did many of the others present, most of which is unprintable. One of his oldest friends, a wrestler named Ernie Minelli, did have this to say about Steve: 'I met him in a gym. We went at it a few times. He knocked out my back tooth once, gave me seven stitches in the mouth and ten in the head. And that's my best friend.'

One of the roasters concluded by saying: 'I've had the pleasure of knowing a man whose name was a household word all over the civilised world ...' Crusher Casey sat listening, smiling and remembering.

In 1986, at the age of seventy-eight, Steve Casey fought his last match – with cancer. Steve lost the match on 11 January 1987 but you can bet that he fought to the end with all his Casey heart.

Later, Steve Casey was one of five people whose portraits were commissioned by the distinguished artist Deirdre O'Connell to be placed in a hall of honour in the village of Sneem. It will provide some insight into the level of respect that Sneem and County Kerry had for Steve Casey to know that one of the others so honoured was George Bernard Shaw, who spent his summers nearby. How far this humble lad had risen. How proud he had been of Kerry and Kerry of him.

It has been mentioned several times in this account that the Casey brothers were very evenly matched in size,

'Steve Casey of Sneem'

The boys of the Kingdom of Kerry,
Seen glory on many a field,
When a football, the green and the gosher
Was the champions of Ireland to yield.

Now brothers called Caseys of Kerry,
A-wrestling was surely their dream,
And the famous of all at the spin, whip or fall,
Is the famous Steve Casey from Sneem.

Steve Casey brought glory to Ireland,
For the champion was surely the cream,
And his fame shall be sung by the old and the young,
Three cheers for the Caseys from Sneem.

When he'd beaten the champions of England,
And the stars of the continent, too,
He next took a trip o'er the ocean,
And came to America, too.

And the Irish came out in the thousands,
While the liner was letting off steam,
And the band they did play,
While the crowd cheered hooray,
Three cheers for Steve Casey from Sneem.

Came the matmen from Texas to Boston,
Came Mazurki, the broth of a boy,
Came the Duseks, the Omaha terror,
Not forgetting old Bibber McCoy.

Came Clark from Dundee who beat Danno,
Sayin' I'll put all you Irish to dream,
Who was finished by Steve, who said here by your leave,
Is revenge for old Ireland and Steve.

When his tour of the U.S. is over,
When the champions have all fallen down,
Sure we'll all go to Cobh for to welcome,
The big man in the green dressing gown.

There'll be bonfires at crossroads in Kerry,
There'll be winin', and dinin', Irene,
And we'll sing all the night, 'til the morning's first light,
Three cheers for Steve Casey of Sneem.

For the Caseys brought luster to Ireland,
And I pledge you this brotherly team,
When their fame shall be sung,
By the old and the young,
Three cheers for the Caseys of Sneem.

> Lyrics to 'Steve Casey of Sneem',
> written in Steve's honour in 1938.

Steve 'Crusher' Casey and family: *Back row (l–r):* Mike, Margaret and
Paddy; *front row (l–r):* Mary, granddaughter Amy and Steve.

strength, stamina and endurance and that they deferred to each other in their judgements of who was 'the best' at anything. It is interesting to note that, at Steve Casey's funeral, his lawyer, a man named Donovan, who had been Steve's best friend for years, passed on these remarks Steve had made before he died. 'He always said that, of the brothers, Tom was the best oarsman and Paddy the best wrestler, but the only man he ever feared, on the water or in the ring, was his younger brother Jim.' Now Steve Casey was a proud man with ample justification and he had never personally made these admissions to any of his brothers. Hearing them, though sadly after Steve was gone from them, created an even firmer bond between these fiercely competitive but also fiercely loyal brothers. Steve's admissions did not belittle or diminish his athletic achievements in his lifetime; rather, they emphasise his humanity and heighten the warmth of his memory in the hearts of his surviving brothers.

TWENTY-ONE

TOM, MICK AND JACK

When we left Tom Casey back in New England, he had given up boxing and followed his brothers into the wrestling arena. The Casey name provided an automatic draw and Tom's talents soon proved equal to the name.

When the United States entered the Second World War, Tom enlisted in the army. In 1943, prior to shipping overseas with his army unit, Tom married a French girl named Bernadette Theriault. Tom's unit was shipped out to Europe, where the Allied armies were pressing hard on the heels of the Germans who were slowly retreating toward their homeland. The Infantry Division to which Tom was assigned was known as the 'Bring 'Em Back Alive' Division, as they were often called upon to conduct operations behind enemy lines and, in particular, to bring back prisoners to be interrogated by intelligence specialists. This was very dangerous duty, indeed, but it became far more perilous when, in December 1944, the Germans mounted their massive counter-attack that was thereafter known as the 'Battle of the Bulge'.

The American army suffered many casualties and had thousands of men captured by the Germans who were pressing to break through the lines and separate the massed forces of Americans and British. But the tiny village of Bastogne held out and its defenders, aided by columns of Patton's Third Army from the South, forced the Germans to give up their attack and to fall back to their original positions. The survivors of this German counter-attack (known as 'The Battered Bastards of Bastogne') suffered from intense cold, lack of shelter, short rations and foul weather, to say nothing of the German tanks and field guns that hammered at them day and night. Tom Casey, it can well be imagined, was not about to be captured or beaten. No mere German army was going to beat a Casey. One can imagine him giving the same answer to the German demand for surrender that was given by General McAuliffe: 'Nuts.' This is not to imply that having a Casey on the American side made the difference between winning and losing that battle but you can bet that it didn't hurt.

After the war, Tom returned to the Boston area. He and Bernadette opened a bar called Tom and Berna's Lounge. In May 1985, Tom succumbed to cancer after fighting a long and courageous battle.

As for Mick Casey: by now, he had entered into a partnership with his brother Paddy in a dance hall in Ealing, London. Paddy was no longer able to wrestle due to the severe back injury he had sustained but he was able to pass on to his brother Mick some of the finer points of wrestling. Mick used these, along with his inborn strength and skill, to sustain him in a wrestling career of some two hundred matches over two decades.

He learned the tricks of the trade quickly from Paddy and began getting matches all over England, Ireland and in many other countries in Europe. He was once matched with the English champion Bert Assirati (whom we have already met) but since Assirati refused to mix it up with Mick and fought a purely defensive type of fight, the match was called a draw. Mick had just started his wrestling career at this point; had he more experience, it is generally agreed he could have overcome Assirati's defensive moves easily. (All the Casey boys were in agreement that a good three years of experience was required to develop 'scientific' wrestling skills.)

One incident in Mick's wrestling career was told with considerable relish by the Casey brothers. It seems that from time to time, wrestlers would meet with the press on their arrival from the United States and claim that, while there, they had beaten either Steve or Jim Casey or both. These claims were totally untrue and enraged the Casey boys in England and in Ireland. On one such occasion, a Dutch wrestler showed up saying that he had beaten both Steve and Jim in the States. He was scheduled for a match in Dublin.

Reading of this man's claims, Paddy drove to Sneem, picked up Mick and drove to Dublin. They arrived at the arena just before the Dutchman was due to begin his match. Mick was dressed in his wrestling togs underneath his coat. Paddy leaped into the ring, grabbed the microphone from the MC and began shouting at the Dutchman: 'You phoney, you claim you beat the Casey brothers in the States. That's a lie and you know it. Here's another Casey brother who is just a beginner at wrestling. You say you can beat the Caseys? You've got to prove that, my friend. Let's see you beat **this** Casey and maybe we'll think about believing you.'

Dancing in London (l–r): Paddy, 'Big Mick' and Mick outside one of Paddy's dance halls in London. The Irish in post-war London will remember Paddy Casey for the entertainment he provided for them at three clubs he established there – the Glocamora in Bayswater, the Innisfree in Ealing Broadway and the Shamrock Club in Elephant and Castle. He began the Glocamora in partnership with fellow Kerryman Bill Fuller but bought him out to become sole owner. He sold his interest in the clubs in the late 1960s.

Mick Casey throwing Bert Assirati across the wrestling ring. Bert Assirati (1908–1990) held the English and European Wrestling Heavyweight titles.

With that, Mick Casey jumped into the ring and threw off his coat. The bewildered Dutchman had very little choice at this point and so the match was on. But it didn't last long – Mick Casey had the Dutchman tied in knots and pinned before he knew what had happened and it was obvious to everyone that his claim of beating Steve and Jim Casey was pure hogwash.

Paddy was the owner of several nightclubs and dance halls in London. Then, as now, occasionally a patron would get rowdy or a fight would break out, so it was considered not only prudent but absolutely essential to have someone on the premises capable of restoring order. Given Mick's reputation for toughness, combined with his reputation as a wrestler, he was the ideal man for Paddy to employ in his clubs.

In a similar situation to the one that prevailed in Boston, there were also some cheap mobster types operating in London who would try to coerce honest businessmen into paying them money for 'protection'. The veiled threat was that if a businessman didn't pay, then fights would be started and trouble caused that might result in the authorities closing down the business.

Now, Paddy had had a wrestling ring installed in his King's Hall Club, in an area where a bar had once stood and he arranged for Mick to give exhibitions of wrestling from time to time for the entertainment of his patrons. One day, three tall, well-built and muscular men came in to Paddy's club and tried to convince him that he should pay them for 'protecting' the place.

'Why the hell should I pay you to protect me?' shouted Paddy. At this moment, Mick walked in. 'Oh, you need us,' one of the men said. 'You need us, all right.'

So Paddy said, 'Look, why don't you show me what you've got to offer in the way of protection? See that fellow over there? One of you should get in the ring with him and show me the kind of protection I'm going to get from you.'

One of the punks swaggered over to the ring and confidently stepped in to confront Mick. Ten seconds later, Mick threw the taller man backwards in a back body drop. This landed the fellow square on his head, knocking him unconscious.

Turning to the next man, Paddy said, 'Well, can you do any better? Show me how you're going to protect me.' So the second man got into the ring with Mick and lasted just about as long as the first: Mick threw him out of the ring bodily.

Continuing to set records with the Casey name *(l–r)*: Paddy's son Steve, Jack's son Steve, a young cousin named Steve (cox for this crew), Jack's son Noel and Paddy's son Patrick.

The third fellow then decided that discretion was the better part of valour, so he hurried out the front door before he could be invited to show his stuff. His two friends followed shortly afterwards, staggering and stumbling out the door.

Mick remained in London until after the war. Shortly thereafter, he married Molly Sullivan from Sneem. They were blessed with two sons, Steve and Mick, and a daughter, Bridie.

Eventually, Mick returned to Sneem and opened Casey's Lounge. Mick also owned the old homestead in Ballaugh, where he was engaged in farming. In addition, he owned and operated no fewer than three dance halls in Leeds and Yorkshire and he opened the first bingo hall ever in the city of Leeds. Quite an enterprising businessman was Mick, as well as a superb athlete.

We had mentioned earlier that Jack Casey remained in Ireland, had married and had taken up farming. He had taken work with a farmer in Mallow, County Cork, and had married his employer's daughter. Together they had a son named Noel Casey. Tragically, Jack's first wife died when Noel was only two or three years old, so Jack returned to the family home at Ballaugh. He helped with the farming and fishing. He built the finest seine boats ever seen in the area and was known as a prodigious fisherman.

After about three years, Jack remarried, this time to Agnes Fitzgerald. They had three sons, Jim, Steve and Paddy. (By now, you will have noted the tendency of the Casey brothers to name their children after one another. This does not make the job of keeping track of the Caseys easier.)

Were the Casey genes still working in Jack's case? Judge for yourself: a superb oarsman in his own right, Jack's son Noel was chosen to coach the English Women's Olympic Rowing Team that competed in the 1984 Olympic events in Los Angeles; Bernie and Caroline, Jack's granddaughters (Noel's daughters), won the singles and pairs at the Henley Regatta in 1984 and were also the All-Ireland Champions, Bernie's children, Jack and Victoria, are carrying on the family legacy in rowing and have competed in England at high levels. What an incredible bloodline.

Jim Casey ventures the opinion that Jack was perhaps the strongest of the seven Casey brothers. He bases this claim in part on the fact that, while still only seventeen or eighteen years old, Jack could lift a huge piece of pig iron that had once been used in a ship's ballast and which lay on the ground near the old boathouse in Sneem. None of the other brothers could match this feat. On a trip back home in 1974, Jim Casey felt compelled to determine just how heavy that ingot really was. He rowed a boat to Sneem where he borrowed an industrial scale. He rowed back to the old boathouse and managed – with some difficulty – to get the ballast on to the scale. It weighed 404 pounds.

TWENTY-TWO

DAN AND PADDY

Dan Casey, you may recall, was the younger by some three years than his nearest brother Tom and was Steve's junior by nearly nine years. So, as his older brothers reached their maturity and went off to seek fame and fortune (which they found in abundance), Dan was left behind with his parents and his sisters. His bout of rheumatic fever when he was about twelve cast a pall over his chances for achieving the athletic greatness that his brothers earned.

However, do you think for one moment that Dan Casey was a weakling? Nothing could be further from the truth. It was no weakling who, at the age of thirteen and not long recovered from a debilitating illness, could pull his weight as he did on the championship tug-of-war team – and pull his weight he literally did. The team coach Mick Sheehan tested each potential team member by having them pull on a rope from which had been suspended a dead weight, hanging on a pulley. As each man was tried out, a stake was driven into the ground to mark the distance that he had moved the weight. Thirteen-year-old Dan's stake was clustered in among those of his older brothers. As for rowing, Jim Casey advances the opinion that Dan was perhaps the finest oarsman in the family, in addition to having done yeoman service as

On 16 May 1993, Dan *(left)* and Jim Casey meet in Dublin for the first time in fifty years.

coxswain in their family rowing triumphs. Jim recalls the time, when Dan was but thirteen, the two of them rowed at Kenmare in the two-oar sweeps against Jerry Shea and a man named Leery. They were two of the finest oarsmen in all of Ireland, yet young Dan and Jim had beaten them by a length.

With all his brothers gone, Dan was forced to row alone. On Jim Casey's holiday in Ireland in 1947, he visited with their old neighbour Pat Leery who lived on the opposite shore. (This fellow had an uncanny knack for predicting weather days in advance. The farmers relied on his intuition when making harvesting plans and he was never known to be wrong.) Pat Leery told Jim Casey that he had lived in his house a long time and had seen Jim's father and his grand-father before him rowing on the water and all the Casey boys as well. He said, in his opinion, Dan Casey was the finest oarsman of all of them. 'He had the most beautiful stroke I've ever seen.'

Said Jim, 'Well then, Pat Leery and how much rowing have you done?'

'Me? Why I've never been in a boat at all.'

Dan never married. While living at Ballaugh, he excelled in building racing boats, at carpentry, bricklaying and stone masonry. He was a born mechanic with a knack for fixing things. Dan parlayed these skills into the development of a construction company that, at its peak, employed over forty men. He built homes in England, France as well as many other countries. Of him, Jim Casey said fondly, 'He was as good as or better than any of the brothers at rowing and at tug-of-war.'

As for Paddy, we had gone a little ahead of ourselves in his case of necessity while recounting his association with his brother Mick. Returning now to his earlier days, we find that Paddy Casey excelled at still **another** sport, one in which his brothers did not participate. That sport was cycling.

Paddy's introduction to cycling came when he was just fifteen years old, when he got a job working for the County

Paddy Casey: winner of many gruelling long-distance cycling races in Ireland. Drawing by Patricia Casey, Paddy's daughter.

Council, which ran the road maintenance programme. The job took him far from home, as he was based in Kenmare, 15 miles from Sneem. He borrowed a bicycle and began cycling to his job assignments. He cycled over all kinds of road surfaces and, at times, over hills and dales that had no roads at all. He was possessed of great stamina and endurance and could ride for hours and never tire.

Paddy entered the cycling competition at the sports field in Sneem one year. One of the competitors was Steven 'Batt' Burns, whom we have already met. You may recall he was the cycling postman who delivered meat to the Casey home from his father's butcher shop in Sneem. By this time, he had become the Irish National Cycling champion.

'Batt' Burns got Paddy to agree to be the 'pacer' in the championship match. The pacer's role was similar to that of a pacer in a long-distance foot race; he would sprint to an early lead in the front of the pack and give the others a pace to work with. After exhausting himself with his sizzling early pace, he would then fall back and be overtaken by the pack. That's what Paddy did the first year and Steven 'Batt' Burns went on to win the race.

Paddy graciously accepted the role of 'pacer' the second year he raced as well. However, he was convinced that if he had not, he could have beaten 'Batt' Burns and all the others with room to spare. It must have cost his competitive soul dearly to agree to such a role.

Later, Paddy entered a gruelling long-distance race several times and won each time. The race was from the bridge in Sneem to a bridge just outside Kenmare, 15 miles away. After cycling from the bridge in Sneem, each contestant signed in at the bridge in Kenmare and cycled back to Sneem, a distance of 30 miles. Paddy proved himself an unbeatable man of iron in these and many races.

While speaking of the earlier days, we must recount that the 1936 Olympics did have some representation from the Casey clan. After having wrestled in the amateur ranks for some two years, Paddy was picked to represent Britain at those 1936 Olympics in Berlin as a light heavyweight. In the national semi-finals, Paddy was beaten by a Turkish wrestler named Abdul. One year later, still wrestling as an amateur, Paddy beat this same Abdul easily, bearing out what the Caseys always said about the value of experience in learning the science of the wrestling profession. The next year saw Paddy enter the professional ranks.

In that same year, 1938, Paddy won the All-Ireland Heavyweight Championship from Tug Wilson of Belfast in a match held at Tolka Park in Dublin.

It was also in 1938, in a match against Jack Sherry at Bellview in Manchester, that Paddy sustained the severe back injury that forced him to give up the sport.

After leaving the wrestling arena, Paddy turned to managing two gyms in London, as well as dance halls in London and the surrounding area.

At about this time an entrepreneur named Bill Fuller persuaded Paddy to go into business with him in his dance halls. Paddy's name was well known in sporting circles and Fuller wanted to use his name to help draw in the crowds. (An interesting sideline concerning Bill Fuller: he was married at that time to a singer who was appearing at his dance halls. Her name was Carmel Quinn and she was to go on to a measure of fame as a regular performer on one of Arthur Godfrey's shows on American television.)

After five or six years of partnership with Fuller, Paddy bought out Fuller's interest in the Glocamora in Bayswater. He worked hard to build up the business and was eminently successful in doing so. Among other innovations, he staged the first 'Irish Rose' contest.

At the time, a rather unique individual named Jack Doyle was working for Paddy. Besides being an Irish tenor, Doyle was a wrestler and a boxer of some repute. (He and his wife both sang at Paddy's club. She was named 'Movita' and later, after divorcing Doyle, was married to Marlon Brando.)

Paddy was interested in arranging a match between his brother Mick and Jack Doyle but Doyle wanted no part of it. Paddy knew that such a match would bring in hordes of people into his club, so he resorted to subterfuge. He arranged for Doyle to wrestle a man named Clem Lawrence, to which Doyle was agreeable. On the same card, he arranged for Mick Casey to wrestle a fellow from South Africa whose name is now forgotten. A day or two before the match, Paddy called both Clem Lawrence and the South African and told them that the matches had been cancelled. So, on the appointed night, only two men showed up on the ring in wrestling trunks: Jack Doyle and Mick Casey. The crowd (many of whom had been let in on the secret so as to ensure a packed house) went wild. This was the match they had all been waiting to see. Doyle was reluctant, to say the least, however, he really had little choice but to face this fearsome gladiator or else suffer the jeers of this bloodthirsty mob. So, the bout was held and Mick won easily, almost anticlimactically.

Paddy Casey had pleased the customers.

Paddy Casey married Agnes Honey in 1942. Agnes was from Piltown, County Kilkenny. They raised three girls and two boys. We have already touched on the dramatic race in which Paddy's two boys, Patrick and Steve, joined their American cousins, Paddy and Mike, at Castletownbere.

Both Patrick and Steve Casey were champion oarsmen. Patrick was a member of the Vesta Rowing Club in London and was an oarsman in the quads that won the 1981 Henley Royal Regatta. Princess Grace of Monaco presented their medals to them. (Strange how the Kellys of Philadelphia entered the lives of the Casey clan several times over the years.)

Paddy's boy, Steve, finished second in the Irish National Championships at Blessington in 1975 and was selected as a member of the Irish International Team to compete in an international regatta to be held in Scotland that same year. However, Steve declined the honour, feeling that he had not been able to take the necessary time to train properly as he was busy running the club. He felt it would not be fair to

Paddy and Agnes with their children, Christmas 1953, (l–r): Patricia, Paddy, Stephen, Bernadette, Agnes, Patrick Jr and Imelda.

Ireland for him to go as their representative if he were not 100 per cent ready. Apparently, finishing second in the Nationals meant, for a Casey, that he just wasn't in proper shape. Both he and his brother benefited from having a fine coach – their father, Paddy.

Paddy and Agnes had a beautiful summer home in Sneem called Kingdom House. It sits on a hillside overlooking the water. The 30 acres that comprise the small estate are beautifully landscaped.

After all those years and all his successful business enterprises, Paddy remained at heart a true sportsman. Reflecting back over the achievements of the Casey brothers, he said, 'Rowing was really our sport. Wrestling was something we did to earn money.'

TWENTY-THREE

FINALLY – THE ASTRONAUTS

Jim and Myrtle Casey hadn't really wanted to go into the kennel business in Texas – the business sought them out. They had settled on one of the pieces of land that Jim had bought – 47 acres in the Alta Loma area. They proceeded to build a home and fenced in part of the land and had kennels built to house Jim's hunting dogs. He was still an avid hunter and a dog trainer as well and kept a stable of some fifty dogs, mostly greyhounds.

Now it happens that NASA's Manned Spacecraft Centre (since renamed the Johnson Space Centre) is located just 20 miles from where the Caseys lived in Alta Loma. In the early 1960s, NASA was engaged in flying the Mercury and Gemini missions, launching the spacecraft from Cape Canaveral in Florida. All the astronauts lived in the area near the Manned Spacecraft Centre, where they worked and trained and they would leave their homes just prior to their assigned missions to fly to Florida, generally taking their families with them to see their launch. Those astronauts with dogs as pets had a problem: the Manned Spacecraft Centre had been built in the coastal prairie around Clear Lake, an area that was sparsely populated at that time. Businesses didn't start to spring up until well after the centre was up and running and

Jim and Myrtle celebrate after one of Jim's great victories.

there were some services that were hard to come by. One of these was a place for the astronauts to board their dogs for the period of time that they and their families were in Florida. There just were no kennels in the area at that time.

In the mid-1960s Jim Casey met Harry Conran, who worked at NASA and who was aware of the astronauts' problem. Knowing of Jim's kennels, Conran asked Jim if he might be willing to put up the astronauts' dogs for a few days while they were off flying in space. Jim readily agreed, so Conran put him in touch with the astronauts' boss, George

Abbey. George was the director of Flight Crew Operations at the centre, the man responsible for selecting and training the astronauts for their hazardous duties. Jim contacted George and confirmed that he would be able to board the astronauts' dogs. The first to bring his dog by was Gene Cernan, who was en route to Cape Canaveral (by then renamed Cape Kennedy) to fly on *Apollo 10*, a critical precursor to the lunar landing, which tested the spacecraft in orbit around the moon prior to the actual landing by *Apollo 11*.

There followed a parade of astronaut dog owners to the Casey kennel in Alta Loma. However, the acreage there really wasn't suitable for a commercial enterprise (remember that Jim hadn't intended it for one when he bought it). The area was low and tended to turn into a mud bog during the rainy season, which, in Texas, was lengthy. To spare his clients from miring their cars in the mud, Jim often had to meet them in his pickup truck at the Busy Bee Café parking lot in nearby Santa Fe, where they would transfer the dogs. Jim finally relocated to some acreage a few miles east in the town of Dickinson, Texas, and there his kennel remains in operation today.

George Abbey was a highly placed, influential man with NASA but was never anything but down to earth in his budding relationship with Jim. Jim was not even aware of the position or title that Abbey held until informed of it by the author who, coincidentally, worked at the Johnson Space Centre for some twenty-four years.

During one of his discussions with Abbey, Jim mentioned his background in the tug-of-war and remarked upon how effective that sport was in building strength. George Abbey

was instantly interested in pursuing this for two reasons: first
and foremost, he was interested in any regimen that would
benefit his team of astronauts as the tug-of-war developed
arm, shoulder and leg strength and also demanded precision
teamwork – his astronauts could not fail to benefit from
such participation; secondly, at that time in Houston, a
concept for physical competitions known as the Highland
Games was forming. These games were being organised by
Texans of English, Irish and Scottish ancestry and would
feature the games played in the 'old countries', including the
tug-of-war. Here was a chance to build up his astronauts
physically, join them in an endeavour requiring teamwork
and provide them with a medium for increasing their *esprit
de corps* by winning at the Highland Games. This was an
undertaking made to order for the likes of George Abbey.
He asked Jim if he would coach a team of astronauts and Jim
agreed. The eager young men showed up for their first
training session at Casey's Kennels, full of youthful fun and
horseplay but Jim, perfectionist that he was, was all business
and no nonsense and soon made it clear to them that he was
their coach and their boss and they either worked hard or
they were off the team. And he said this to the cream of the
crop of America's young men – the astronaut corps! But they
listened and they obeyed.

Jim put together two teams – one heavyweight and one
light heavyweight. He bossed them around as if they were
recruits in boot camp and they watched in awe as he
demonstrated the great strength he still had, even though he
was approaching seventy years of age – and they learned.

They called their teams 'The Ace Moving Company' and
had the name printed on their T-shirts. The derivation of the

name is a little obscure: By that time, NASA was well into the Space Shuttle programme and on one of these missions, a trio of playful astronauts, having successfully completed the task of launching one spacecraft into orbit and retrieving from orbit another malfunctioning communications satellite which they returned to earth for repair and reuse, posed for their still and television cameras while still in orbit holding up a sign which proclaimed them to be the 'Ace Moving Company'.

Well, the 'Ace Moving Company' with Jim Casey's coaching, proved that they could move more than free-floating satellites – they moved all the competing tug-of-war teams they faced over the centre line, digging in their heels and pulling mightily, with Jim Casey on the sidelines shouting instructions and words of encouragement.

They came up against teams of firemen, policemen, college athletes from nearby Rice University and a team of wrestlers. They beat them all. Neither team was beaten over a three-year period.

Here are some of the names of the astronauts who pulled for Jim Casey:

Admiral Richard Truly was a pilot in the early approach and landing testing of the orbiter, in which the unpowered vehicle was released from the back of a 747 carrier aircraft to test the flight controls and aerodynamic stability of the craft. He went on to command shuttle missions and, after the *Challenger* tragedy, he was rapidly promoted until he became the top man at NASA, the NASA Administrator.

Navy Captain Bob Crippen, the pilot who, along with John Young, crewed the first launch of the shuttle in

April 1981. He was the Director of the Space Shuttle programme in Washington D.C.

Other astronaut members were Jack Lousma, Dr Richard Thornton and Tim Kincaid, as well as the afore-mentioned George Abbey (who is a former Associate NASA Administrator in Washington), Harry Conran and Jim Casey's son, Steve.

They were all winners in their own right and in their own fields and under the tutelage of Jim Casey, they all became winners at tug-of-war, a sport which none of them had ever tried before. They **had** to become champions – Jim Casey would never tolerate any losing.

Apart from his kennels and coaching teams of astronauts in the tug-of-war, one of Jim's principal activities takes him back to his earliest roots in County Kerry – rowing.

Almost single-handedly, Jim excited an interest in rowing in his part of Texas. He was involved in the operation of a rowing club at the South Shore Harbour Marina on Clear Lake, just outside the Johnson Space Centre. This club, which boasts 300 members and a floating dock measuring 75 feet in length and 35 feet in width, has between forty and fifty boats of all kinds – singles, doubles, four-oar sweeps – for rent or for sale. A second, smaller facility, the Bay Area Rowing Club, is situated on the opposite (northern) side of the lake. Jim coached members at both clubs.

Speaking of coaching, Jim designed and built a most unique training facility in the back garden of his home in Dickinson, Texas. It consists of a replica of the interior of a racing scull built in at ground level, complete with oarlocks

Jim Casey instructs astronaut Jim Weatherbee on rowing in his unique back garden 'cabana'.

and sliding seats. This 'boat' is covered by a roof. The two sidewalls of the structure are of glass, installed in movable sections that can be raised vertically to permit the oars of the 'boat' to be extended. The sections can be raised or lowered depending on the oar clearance of the individual student. Jim constructed two more such facilities for other rowing coaches in Texas.

Jim's property backs on to a 26-acre lake. Jim designed and had built a stable dock from which racing boats can be boarded and often gave instruction on this body of water in boats that he kept in a small boathouse on his property.

One of the boats in this shed is the subject of some intense nostalgia. A single shell of sleek mahogany, it hangs, gleaming, upon wall hooks in the boathouse. Its lines and design speak of days past and indeed they should, for this is the very boat in which Jim Casey broke the course record, along with Tom and Steve, on the Charles River in November 1940.

TWENTY-FOUR

BACK TO SNEEM

The story of the incredible Casey brothers has now been told. All of the essential facts – and again I repeat, every story in this book is well documented.

There are dozens of sideline stories, amusing anecdotes and the like which might have been included but which were not since they are secondary to the central thrust of the book, which is to tell of the unbelieveable athletic feats of these seven remarkable men. They accomplished so much, each of them, that their stories need no dressing or embellishment.

One significant fact that has not been overlooked, and which bears noting here, is that all three of the brothers who went to America – Steve, Tom and Jim – eventually became American citizens. It is hard to say whether the Casey boys or the United States of America benefited more from their naturalisation. Most assuredly though, the US gained three of the most competitive and rugged citizens that they could ever have hoped for.

Though these three became Americans and most of the others lived or worked or competed elsewhere for most of their lives, their hearts remained where their hearts and souls had been formed in the beautiful County of Kerry.

To County Kerry they returned, to effect a Casey reunion, in the summer of 1983. All the Casey brothers were living then and five of them, Steve, Jim, Paddy, Jack and Mick, were able to travel to Sneem and to Ballaugh. Tom was too ill in Boston to travel and Dan could not leave England at that time.

However, the five Casey brothers who assembled there in Ballaugh and who took to the four-oar gig again in the Sneem Regatta relived memories of triumph of fifty years past. All were over seventy years of age and each had achieved enviable records of athletic achievement, which this book has attempted to chronicle. What an amazing group of athletes.

The crowds of people lining the shore at the regatta in Sneem on that August day in 1983 were treated to a sight that few have ever been privileged to see.

Easing their bodies into the boat, the five Casey brothers settled in to their positions and grasped the oars in that same classic style that had marked their performance fifty years earlier. Paddy's back injury precluded his rowing, so he took the coxswain's position. Steve took the stroke oar, Jim was number three, Mick number two and Jack was in the bow. They pushed off and began rowing. Those on the shore who were old enough and lucky enough to have been present when the Caseys won the Salter Challenge Cup many years before were taken back to that day by what they saw.

Although they had not been together in a boat for fifty years, the brothers still rowed as one. Their oars broached and cleared the water in perfect unison. Backs erect, arms outstretched, they propelled the boat through the shimmering water as smoothly as a raindrop sliding down silk.

Four of the Casey brothers who reunited for a rowing challenge fifty years after their historic win over the Whiddy crew at the Killarney Regatta, *(l–r):* Steve, Jim, Mick and Jack.

Many of those crowding the shoreline found it difficult to cheer because of the lumps that formed in their throats. They knew they were watching the final performance of the greatest oarsmen and the greatest individual athletes that Ireland had ever seen.

As for the Casey brothers themselves – they knew it too. And not withstanding the good-natured bantering, joshing and playful threatening they engaged in, they shared a feeling that was at once sad and proud: sad that they would probably

Five Casey brothers reunite in Sneem in 1983. The boat is the one they raced in as young men. Proud they were to be the Caseys: the toughest family on earth.

never meet this way again, in a display of their combined physical prowess, and proud to reflect on what they, the seven Casey boys from Sneem, had accomplished both individually and as a team of brothers over the long and eventful years of their lives.

POSTSCRIPT

16 January 1982: The seven Casey brothers from Sneem, County Kerry, were inducted into the Irish Sports Hall of Fame. They were the only family ever so honoured and it is very likely that they will be the last.

Sporting Legends: Paddy Casey *(left)* accepts the Hall of Fame Award on behalf of the Casey family, presented by Ronnie Delany. In his day, Ronnie Delany had no equal and won gold for the 1,500 metre event in 1956 at the Olympic games in Melbourne, Australia.

A TRIBUTE FROM THE CASEY BROTHERS

While the contents of this book were designed to tell the story of the incredible Casey brothers from Sneem in County Kerry, they wished to acknowledge that other gifted athletes were active in the area and asked the author to find a way to include them in this book so as to provide some measure of recognition. The members of the Kerry football team, in particular, were fondly remembered by the Casey boys. They used to row 10 miles across Kenmare Bay, walk 5 miles further to the playing field and then would buy food with the entrance money their mother had given them while depending on their ability to find a handy perch on a hill or by partially scaling the wall surrounding the field to see the match. The boys idolised the Kerry team, which was seldom beaten and which won more All-Ireland titles in football than any other county.

Their members were:

Mick O'Dwyer	Waterville
Mick O'Connell	Valentia
Jack O'Shea	Caherciveen
John Egan	Tahilla, Sneem
Mickey 'Ned' O'Sullivan	Kenmare
Pat, Mick and Tom Spillane	Templenoe
Eoin 'Bomber' Liston	Waterville
Micksie Palmer	Sneem
Fitzgerald brothers	South Square, Sneem
John Joe Sheehey	Tralee

The Thames Rowing Club crew, London, who represented Great Britain in the 1981 World Rowing Championships included two Casey sisters, Caroline and Bernie, and the crew was coached by their father, Noel, (l–r): Sue Brown (cox), Jane Cross, Sarah Hunter Jones (who rowed in the 1984 Olympics), Caroline Casey, Bernie Casey and Michael Hanrahan (one of the sponsors).

Other area athletes whom the Casey brothers wanted to include are:

EDDIE MULCAHEY	All-Ireland Senior Champion Weight Thrower – Sneem
DR PAT O'CALLAHAN	From Kanturk, County Cork, he won gold medals for hammer throwing in the 1928 and 1932 Olympic Games.
DANNO O'MAHONEY	Wrester who also wrestled in the United States

INDEX

Numbers in **bold** indicate photographs